A History of County Cricket

MIDDLESEX

A History of County Cricket

MIDDLESEX

E. M. Wellings

Arthur Barker Limited
5 Winsley Street London W1

ISBN 0 213 16403 5
Printed in Great Britain by
Bristol Typesetting Co. Ltd., Bristol

Contents

Illustrations

The photographs in this book are reproduced by kind permission of the Press Association Ltd. The author and publishers would also like to thank Sport and General Press Agency Ltd for the photograph of Jack Robertson.

1 Walkers and First Hearne

Over-arm bowling was legalized, W. G. Grace began his first-class career, Wisden produced the first edition of his *Almanack*, and Middlesex formed their county club. Those events made the year 1864 significant in the history of cricket. The fame of the new club was established by its wealth of amateurs. Perhaps no other county has been represented by so many, which explains why their batting in the past was usually more famous than their bowling. Moreover, possessing no dour professional batsmen in their early days, such as the northern counties had with Barlow, who once batted two hours and a half for 5 runs, Scotton and Louis Hall, they rapidly gained a reputation for playing attractive cricket. Their own great professional batsmen of later date, from the whirlwind Trott to Compton and Edrich, were mostly cast in the same cavalier mould as the amateurs.

Denis Compton, with his gift for improvisation, was the direct descendant of the early batsmen, of whom the Walkers of Southgate were originals. Isaac Donnithorne Walker's favourite stroke was the drive over cover-point's head. His brother Russell had his own means of dealing with what came to be called bouncers or bumpers. He struck them over his left shoulder and high over the long-stop fielder to the boundary. Thomas Hearne, the most distinguished professional of Middlesex's early years, was the last successful employer of the ancient stroke known as the draw. This in effect was a leg glance but played between the body and the stumps. By that time most batsmen had discarded the stroke, having found that the odds against tickling the ball into the leg-stump, directly or via the right pad, were not good enough to render it a profitable gamble. Hearne seems to have avoided those traps more regularly than most. If he sometimes played on, his gamble was as nothing to that of Nigel Haig many years later, when he executed a late cut perfectly, but from such an improbable position that the ball uprooted the leg stump.

Teams had represented Middlesex before the county club was formed. In 1830 their match with Marylebone Cricket Club was the first in which no-balls were recorded. However, 1864 is the official starting point, with John Walker as the first vice-president and two of his brothers on the committee. Except when dismissed by 20 by MCC that year, the new club fully held its own. There were seven Walker brothers, the first of many family groups contributing to the Middlesex story. Among others were the Hearnes, the Studds, the Lytteltons, the Beldams, the Manns, the Fords, four Douglas brothers, the Hendrens and the Comptons. Six of the seven Walkers represented the Gentlemen against the Players, the exception being the second, Alfred, who was an exceptionally fast under-arm bowler. They must have been tough, for it was usual for them to bat without pads even on the then rough and bumpy pitches. I. D. wore pads only if a fast bowler, such as George Freeman of Yorkshire, was in the opposition to threaten his shins too greatly.

I. D. succeeded his brother Vyell Edward and was the team's captain until 1887, when at the age of 43 he handed on to A. J. Webbe. He, the youngest, V. E. and R. D. were the most distinguished of the brotherhood. They were primarily fast-scoring batsmen but were fully qualified also as all-rounders, Isaac and Vyell bowling lobs and Russell being a slow round-arm bowler. Isaac played a great innings of 165 for the Gentlemen against the Players in 1868, in which he hit two sixes, three fives, seventeen fours and ten threes. Vyell first played for the Gentlemen at the age of 19. Three years later, playing for England against Surrey, his lobs took all ten wickets in the first innings, and he had scores of 20 not out and 108. He took all ten in an innings three times in first-class cricket.

County cricket was about to flourish. Until the middle sixties touring teams of leading players, mainly professionals, played most of the important cricket. Now the All England XI, the United England XI and the South of England XI were approaching the end of their period of prosperity. Dissensions in William Clarke's All England XI had led to the formation of the breakaway United England concern; the birth of the South of England XI resulted from a similar cause. It was a troubled world into which the Middlesex club was launched, for the quarrelling among the professionals affected the county game also. In particular the ill feeling between north and south professionals upset teams for numerous matches. The two leading counties, Surrey and Nottinghamshire, quarrelled so violently that they did not play each other for several seasons. Middlesex, being predominantly amateur, were not closely affected. The game was more peaceful in the seventies, when half a dozen different sides headed the county tables. Gloucestershire, thriving on W. G. and his brothers, were now a power in the land, and Yorkshire had passed through their period of turmoil, during which groups of players refused to take part in matches if others were selected. In the eighties Nottinghamshire were the great side, the Notts of Arthur Shrewsbury, William Gunn and William Attewell. Surrey's turn came in the next decade when they had Bobby Abel, Tom Hayward, Walter Read, Maurice Read, George Lohmann and the great fast-bowling combination of Richardson and Lockwood. Only then did inter-county games dominate first-class cricket. Until the championship was recast in 1895 12 such matches in a season was a large ration. By the end of 1869 W. G. had already made 11 100s in first-class cricket, but his first for Gloucestershire did not arrive until 1870, and more than half his first hundred centuries were scored for other sides.

It is difficult to form an accurate picture of cricket at that time. Batting we know, was based on forward play, for Shrewsbury, who began for Nottinghamshire in 1875, is credited with having developed back-foot play. When the Middlesex club was formed, a batting average in the 20s was good. E. M. Grace, elder brother of W.G., had created something of a sensation when he averaged 35 from 27 innings in 1863. Three years later W.G. and V. E. Walker each had an average of 42, but only six others exceeded 30. For years to come the bowlers had the more striking figures. In 1867 Tom Emmett of Yorkshire headed their list with 5.36, and thirteen years later the 177 wickets of Alfred Shaw of Notts cost only 8.1 each. As late as 1890 four bowlers, headed by Lancashire's Johnny Briggs, averaged under 13.

Playing success came to the new county quickly. Two years after their formation they were ranked as the top county, having twice beaten Surrey by an innings and also having defeated Lancashire twice. Six of their eight county matches were won and the others drawn. Vyell Walker headed the batting averages with 52, which was an exceptional figure in the playing conditions of the time. Hearne averaged 35 with the bat and 13 with the ball, and a migrant bowler from Nottingham, Hewitt, contributed materially to the success. Hewitt represented both Nottinghamshire and Middlesex that season, a not uncommon practice, which means that it is unrealistic to date the county championship further back than 1873, the reason being that in that year qualification rules were adopted for the first time. A player then had to decide at the start of each season whether he would represent the county of his birth or residence. Even then no points-scoring system was laid down to decide the order of the nine counties concerned: Derbyshire, Gloucestershire, Kent, Lancashire, Middlesex, Nottinghamshire, Surrey, Sussex and Yorkshire. There was, therefore, sometimes a lack of general agreement about which county were champions until 1895, when the competition was organized with fourteen of the seventeen present-day first-class counties, excluding only Worcestershire, Northamptonshire and Glamorgan.

Though Middlesex were successful on the field, they were not for several years quite sure what field it would be. Officially they had three grounds. The first was rented from an Islington innkeeper, who also started using it in 1868 for races and fêtes. The condition of their second ground at West Brompton was so bad that in two years they played only one home match on it. Then for four seasons they played at Prince's, near Harrods, but they were not well suited. All this time they were being wooed by M C C with offers of Lord's. They did not think their finances would allow them to accept, but late in 1876 they decided to take a chance. It was agreed to play four matches at Lord's during the following season, when they would take all the gate money and be responsible for all expenses. The move was an immediate financial success, and also a playing one, for two years later Middlesex were unbeaten in six county matches and were generally considered to have taken the championship to Lord's for the first time. In that way Middlesex became closely associated with M C C and have remained tenants at cricket's headquarters ever since.

The Walkers had continued to be the backbone of the side in the meantime. Now Webbe, Walter Hadow and two Lytteltons had joined the side. The Hon Edward Lyttelton, with 29.25, was fourth in the English batting averages in 1878 to Selby, Ulyett and W. G. Grace. Alexander Josiah Webbe played his only Test that year against Australia, but his greatest year was 1887, after he had taken over the Middlesex captaincy, when he averaged 47. At the beginning of August he scored 192 not out against Kent and a week later 243 not out on a fiery pitch against Yorkshire. Webbe, who had a crouching stance, was not such a free stroke player as most Middlesex amateurs of the period. He was, however, more consistent than most.

The Hon Alfred Lyttelton was the most celebrated of his family, whose most recent cricketing son, the present Lord Cobham, captained Worcestershire before the Second World War. Alfred Lyttelton was a wicket-keeper and a very aggressive batsman. He was also once England's most successful bowler, when Australia made 551 at the Oval in 1884 and all 11 Englishmen bowled. Grace took over behind the stumps, and Lyttelton, bowling lobs, took the last four wickets for 19. A year earlier in the Middlesex side he and Isaac Walker had scored 324 for the second wicket in a total of 537 against Gloucestershire at Bristol. Grace took one wicket for 154 and he and the other bowlers suffered greatly in one spell of 100 minutes, during which Walker and Lyttelton slammed 220.

In the early eighties Charles Studd shone brilliantly for Middlesex and England as an all-rounder. In 1882 and 1883 he did the double, played five times against Australia and then retired at a very early age to become a missionary. The double of 1,000 runs and 100 wickets had been done only six other times, five of them by W. G. Studd's brother, G. B., also played for England. Among the many amateurs of the period who also contributed conspicuously, if sometimes in erratic fashion, were H. R. Bromley-Davenport, C. J. Ottaway, T. Case, J. J. Sewell,

G. F. H. Leslie, G. F. Vernon, S. W. Scott, fast bowler A. F. G. Ford and Charles Inglis Thornton, one of the game's mightiest hitters. When he was eighteen he began his innings for Eton against Harrow by driving the ball straight over the old pavilion at Lord's and into the garden beyond. Later he made the hit at Scarborough for which he is best remembered. Batting at the pavilion end, he drove a ball straight. It carried the houses and pitched in the square beyond. Until the Australian all-rounder Pepper made a comparable drive in an end-of-war Festival match there, nobody else had ever hit the ball into the square, and Pepper's clout reached it via the houses. Thornton landed the ball in the square without touching anything on the way. That hit, which was in the course of a whirlwind 107 not out (containing eight sixes, twelve fours, two twos and seven singles) could not be measured. Several were, and his longest from bat to landing place was one of 168 yards at Brighton.

Thornton was a consistent smiter. In 1871, when he was 21, he began his innings for Cambridge University against the Gentlemen of England by hitting his first ball for six, the next two for four each and the fourth for another six. In the same year he made 31 in 16 minutes and 61 in 47 for the Gentlemen of the South against the Players of the South. It seems incongruous that such an aggressive batsman should have bowled lobs. The number of such bowlers still in the game, and flourishing, is no less curious, for round-arm bowling had been legal since 1828, and over-arm was as old as the Middlesex Club.

A little later came Sir Timothy O'Brien, bringing to Middlesex batting all the dash of the Irish. An innings of 119 against Gloucestershire, followed by two quick-fire knocks against the foe at the Oval, established his fame, and in 1889 he walloped an unbeaten 100 in only 80 minutes off the Yorkshire bowlers. He played for England against Australia, and so did A. P. Lucas, who broke his journey from Surrey to Essex at Lord's to play for Middlesex and to take a high place in the national averages with 33.4 in 1883. A large contribution was also made to Middlesex – and England – by Gregor MacGregor.

The flow of amateurs was continuous, and shortly Andrew Ernest Stoddart, who was born in the same year as the county club, was to come on the scene. In 1886 he hit 485 for Hampstead, when they made 813 for nine wickets in a single day against the Stoics. The next year he played in the Centenary Match at Lord's and scored 151 for England against MCC. He was the leading Middlesex batsman of his time and in the nineties played 16 times against Australia. He had two centuries and a Test average of 35 with an aggregate of 996 – fine scoring, even allowing for a now steady improvement in the standard of the pitches.

Professionals were still few. Thomas Hearne and Hewitt had done their bit. They were succeeded by George Burton, who was the backbone of their attack throughout the eighties. In ten years he took 504 wickets for under 17 runs each for a county averaging no more than 11 matches a season. He was a slow-medium bowler, as was West, another professional, who played for a time. A third professional was Spillman, a batsman-stumper, but his first-class career was very short.

All three played in 1886, when Middlesex went as close as they have ever been to defeating an Australian touring team. Spillman made 87 and, with J. G. Walker who also did quite well, making 67, pulled the Middlesex team round after they had made a bad start. Even so they were nearly 100 behind, 259 for 153, and despite 60s by Webbe and Scott they could set the Australians only 123 in the final innings. Burton, who had taken eight wickets for 136 in the first innings, and West almost snatched the match. The Australians were at the half-way mark with only two wickets down when West joined Burton in the attack. They quickly took the next seven, helped by some fine catching, and at 120 for nine wickets the Australians still needed three runs. Blackham, their stumper, who was also a useful batsman, got them, but Burton finished triumphantly with six wickets for 56 while West took three for 25.

Two years later Burton took all ten Surrey wickets in the first innings at the Oval for 59, and he helped Middlesex to beat Nottinghamshire, the leading county of the period, for the first time in 22 years. The victory for which they had waited so long was overwhelming, the margin an innings and 55 runs. Their record against Surrey was very different. Up to the time of the reorganization of the championship in 1895 it was level pegging between the London rivals.

From that time the professional element in the side became more and more important, even if amateurs continued to be the larger force numerically. In 1888 their greatest bowler, J. T. Hearne, played for the first time against the Australians and dismissed two first-line batsmen. He did not play at all in the following season, but in 1890 he played regularly and was immediately mowing down the leading batsmen. He began by taking six wickets for 62 against Nottinghamshire, the reigning champions, and his victims included Arthur Shrewsbury, the greatest professional batsman of the nineteenth century, and stonewaller Scotton. He then bowled against Gloucestershire and dismissed both W. G. and E. M. Grace. Against the Australians of that year he took five for 42 and three for 49, and the touring captain, W. L. Murdoch, fell to him in both innings.

Hearne must be counted among the greatest quick-medium bowlers of all time, ranking in English cricket history with Maurice Tate and Alec Bedser, with Sidney Barnes out in front. He had a fine flowing action, and there was still rhythm in his delivery when, in his early 60s, he used to coach us at Oxford before the start of the University season. His bowling was based on the offbreak. Today anyone who imparts such spin at above slow-medium pace is said to bowl offcutters. Perhaps they do, but bowlers of medium and above formerly used genuine finger-spin. It is a modern theory that such spin is possible only to slow bowlers. Bedser was said to have a legcutter. In fact he also used genuine finger-spin, which was imparted to the ball by the third finger of his bowling hand.

From the time he started until the outbreak of the First World War Hearne stayed immovable in the county side, and for England he took 49 Test wickets in 12 matches. At the start his professional bowling partners were Rawlin and Phillips. Then he was teamed in succession with two Australians, Albert Trott and Frank Tarrant. He exceeded 200 wickets in all first-class cricket in three of his first ten seasons. He did the hat-trick four times. He is one of only four bowlers who have passed 3,000 wickets. The others were all slow bowlers, Wilfred Rhodes, Tich Freeman and Charlie Parker. For Middlesex alone between 1891 and 1898 he took 924 wickets at a cost of under 16 runs each, and his career average was under 18. The batting opposition he faced was formidable and became even stronger in the new century. In matches against Australian touring teams he was at his best. In 1896, representing M C C, Middlesex and the South, he had figures of four wickets for 4, nine for 73, six for 41, four for 19 and six for 8 against Harry Trott's side, and in 1899 he did the hat-trick in a Test at the expense of Clem Hill, Monty Noble and Sid Gregory.

After their success in 1878 Middlesex did not hold top position until well after the reformation of the championship. Indeed after their first championship they had a comparatively lean spell and did not challenge the leaders closely. Yet they had their triumphs, and these were not restricted to their victory over Nottinghamshire at the 23rd attempt, and some good results against Surrey. In 1889 they gained a thrilling win against Yorkshire when left under three hours to make 280. O'Brien hit 100 in only 80 minutes, and Middlesex cantered home with time in hand. In 1891 they rose to third place, the Yorkshire-born Rawlin batting and bowling with considerable success, and Stoddart hitting 215 not out against Lancashire. That was their only score of over 200 before the championship was enlarged, just as Hearne's 212 – in all first-class cricket – two years afterwards was the only instance where a Middlesex man took more than 200 wickets. Such performances became steadily less common. In that same season they triumphed over Surrey after following on 179 behind. Stoddart and O'Brien made 228 for the first wicket. Then F. G. J. Ford, the most distinguished of three brothers, a left-hander and another of the game's ferocious hitters, slammed 74. Finally Hearne and Rawlin skittled Surrey for 119. The 1894 season was, in a bowling sense, all Hearne and Rawlin, who had his best season – 90 wickets cheaply for the county and 104 altogether. No other bowler took as many as 20 wickets. Cricket had passed through its Middle Ages, and modern history was ushered in by the Reformation of the championship.

2 Men of the Golden Age

What has been called the Golden Age of cricket was close at hand. I saw no cricket before 1919, and my close connection with the first-class game did not start until 1928 at Oxford. Yet I accept that description of the past age. It was surely the most exciting period in which to have played. That much was made obvious to my generation, when midway between the wars we played with or against or watched the then elderly survivors from that time. There was Frank Woolley with his nonchalant, cavalier brand of batting, which always carried the fight to his bowling opponents. There was George Gunn, whose batting seemed to recognize no rules and who played as the mood moved him, sometimes scoring only off good balls and scorning the bad ones. There was Rhodes with his bewildering command of flight. And there was Jack Hobbs, the master batsman who was still enthralling to watch, and yet was said by his contemporaries to have been much more so in his young days, when he played many daringly improvised strokes. If such cricketers were a fair sample of how the game was played by them and such brilliant amateurs as Stanley Jackson and Ranjitsinhji in the years before 1914, the claim that it was the Golden Age cannot easily be refuted.

Middlesex entered the new era with Hearne and Rawlin and their squad of amateur batsmen, headed by Stoddart, O'Brien, Ford, MacGregor and R. S. Lucas, who the season before had shared a ninth-wicket stand of 150 with Rawlin at the Oval. They were now joined by four who would play leading roles in the Middlesex story. Plum Warner began in 1895. So did James Douglas, who became a most reliable opening batsman, and C. M. Wells, a slow bowler then in the Cambridge University side. The fourth was the consistent H. B. Hayman. Yet with all this

18

talent Middlesex fortunes were curiously mixed. They were wont to 'yo-yo' up and down the championship table. They were an erratic side and unpredictable, collectively and individually.

The most unpredictable individual action was surely that of a highly-gifted young fast bowler named Sidney Webb. Starting in 1897 with a flourish, he took ten Nottinghamshire wickets for 101. He then back-pedalled until he resumed with similar flourish in two seasons for Lancashire, for whom he qualified by residence. At that point, with fame beckoning him, he decided to become a slow leg break bowler, and that was his end.

Even Hearne had his ups and downs. Perhaps it was the result of playing in unpredictable company. Near the start of the new century he seemed to be slipping back, but came again to play a large part in the winning of the championship before suffering a second slump. Just when he was being written off after some fairly lean years he recaptured his old form in 1910 and finished top of the national averages, his 129 wickets costing fewer than 13 runs each. He was still going strong when the war came in 1914. That ended his championship career, when he was 47, but nine years later he played one more first-class match against Scotland. No bowler of pace has ever lasted as long in first-class company.

Under the new championship regime Hearne and Rawlin saw the county off to a good start. They beat Nottinghamshire twice, and against Sussex O'Brien, who passed 200, and Lucas scored at 100 an hour while making 338 for the fifth wicket. That is one of the two stands from the nineteenth century that still remain unequalled among the county's records. The other came four years later, when R. W. Nicholls and W. Roche, who were otherwise comparatively undistinguished, made their contribution to history by scoring 230 for the tenth wicket at Lord's in only two hours and a half, after Kent had taken the first nine for 55.

Roche, like Trott and Tarrant, was an Australian from Victoria. The importation of such cricketers was not entirely welcomed elsewhere. In the 1898 *Wisden* the editor, Sydney Pardon, commented on the presence of Trott, Roche and O'Halloran on the M C C ground staff, with the object of qualifying them for Middlesex. He recorded that this had aroused 'some ill feeling and dissatisfaction among the other counties'. O'Halloran came to nothing, and Roche did so little as a slow bowler that his time in championship cricket was short. The other counties, except Kent who suffered from Roche's number 11 batsmanship, had no cause to be dismayed about him and O'Halloran. Trott was a very different proposition.

Trott was the Jekyll and Hyde of the game. For three or four years after joining the county side his all-round play was tremendous. He was the first man to top 1,000 runs and 200 wickets in a season. He did so both in 1899 and 1900. Only three other all-rounders have done that double: Alec Kennedy of Hampshire, Maurice Tate, who did so three times, and George Hirst, who outdid them all with his 2,385 runs and 208 wickets in 1906. 'Original' is the word commonly used to describe Trott's bowling by his contemporaries, including C. B. Fry and Plum Warner.

Fry wrote: 'On the whole he may be regarded as the most original, inventive and enterprising performer with the ball at present engaged in first-class cricket.' Warner wrote similarly, praising particularly his 'wonderful fast yorker, which was really fast and almost invariably straight'. Trott, it seems, bowled everything from slow to fast. His arm when delivering the ball was sometimes brushing his ear and at others almost in a round-arm position. *Wisden*'s summing up probably classified this erratic genius most accurately: 'Perhaps he may best be described as a pace bowler.' Not a fast, nor a slow, nor a spin, nor a swing bowler, but a pace bowler, and the meaning was very different from, and more literal than, its meaning now, when all between gentle-medium and express are categorized as pace bowlers.

Trott was no less original and inventive with the bat. He was a powerfully-built man who delighted in weighty hitting. In the first of his great years, 1899, he drove a ball straight over the present pavilion at Lord's. He is still the only man who has carried the pavilion. Others have landed on the roof, including Frank Mann and Hendren, or on the top deck, including Fred Trueman, during an exhibition match, staged when a Test match had suffered an early death and a Saturday crowd had to be entertained. But none has matched Trott's mighty drive. He might have been better off if he had never made it. Subsequently he seemed to be trying for similar fame wherever Middlesex played, and his batting record suffered from his lack of discretion. In addition Trott was outstanding as a fielder in the slips, where his vast hands grabbed everything in reach.

After those two tremendous seasons Trott was soon in decline and never achieved the double again. By 1905 he had gone back so far that *Wisden* lamented that 'Trott went from bad to worse. We cannot help thinking that he would be all the better for a little hard training during the winter and spring.' He was at 32 still a young man with time to recover, four years younger than Hearne, who was still able to take 100 wickets a season at the outbreak of war, four years after Trott retired.

Trott came again only in 1907, when he put his name once more in the record books by brilliant bowling in his Benefit match. It came in the second innings, when Lionel Palairet, Len Braund and P. R. Johnson had given Somerset a fair start towards scoring the necessary 264 for a win. Trott took four wickets in as many balls and almost made it five in five. Then he also did a second hat-trick, finished with seven for 20 and gave Middlesex the victory by 166 runs. Trott described the feat as akin to bowling himself into the workhouse. In fact, since the match was then in its final innings, the effect on the gate-takings could not have been all that serious. Three years later Trott dropped out of county cricket, and in 1914 he died at the age of 41.

Frank Tarrant was an even greater acquisition. He was the greatest of the several cricketers from overseas who have played for Middlesex. They include the wicket-keeper, Halliwell, A. E. Vogler and an all-rounder, Owen-Smith, from South Africa, Dr Gunasekera from Ceylon and yet another Australian recently in Alan Connolly. Halliwell and Vogler, in fact, each played only one match, but the latter made his a good one. Vogler had scores of 52 and 35 and took five wickets for 91 with his googlies in 1906.

Tarrant's first season, in 1905, evoked little interest outside the county. It was just a steady start at the age of 23. His batting average was just over 27, his bowling just under. Soon, however, he was reeling off the double season after season. He did it eight times in all and, if the First World War had not ended his cricket in England when he was still a young man, he would surely have come much closer to Rhodes and Hirst, who did the double 16 and 14 times repectively. He was generally accepted as being bracketed with Hirst as the greatest all-rounder of his period. More than ten years after his last match for Middlesex he returned to Australia from a long spell of cricketing in India. He played so well against Arthur Gilligan's touring team that he was even then near Test selection. That he did not return in 1919 was a serious loss to the county.

Unlike Trott, Tarrant was a studious batsman. He was sometimes accused of being too cautious in his early years. From a quiet start he progressed towards enterprise, and at the end of the era he was a hard-driving batsman. His left-arm spin bowling was deadly if there was the least help in the pitch. In his ten years Tarrant had a magnificent record for Middlesex, with more than 12,000 runs, including 26 centuries, and an average of 38, and more than 1,000 wickets at 17.4 each. His complete record in English cricket was 15,903 runs and 1,335 wickets. Only as a fielder could Trott be claimed as his superior. When the war ended Tarrant in India underlined the loss Middlesex suffered from his absence, when he emulated Vyell Walker, W. G. Grace and E. M. Grace by scoring a century and taking all ten wickets in an innings in a first-class match.

Rawlin, much more a batsman of consequence than a bowler in his later years, was still playing when Tarrant arrived. Indeed he was still playing an occasional game as late as 1909, when he was 52. He took 100 wickets once in a first-class season, and he waited until he was 42 before making his only century. That it was then scored against Middlesex's great rivals, Surrey, doubtless made it all the sweeter. Yet as a painstaking batsman and valuable foil to Hearne he was an important member of the side for many years. Phillips was not so long in the side, but from the arrival of Hearne the county were never without a sound nucleus of professional bowling. The third Hearne, young Jack, was to come along with his leg breaks before the period ended – together with Patsy Hendren – and from 1905 to 1913 Mignon took 410 wickets for Middlesex as a fast bowler.

For most of the 20 years after the championship was reformed Bosanquet and C. M. Wells were the only amateur bowlers to achieve much. Wells was a schoolmaster able to play only in the closing stages of each season. As Middlesex usually arranged their programme to include as much cricket as possible in August he was able to play several matches. Such was their emphasis on matches late in the season that in 1898 they did not start their championship programme until 30 May. Wells regularly helped the professionals by taking around 25 wickets with his slows, and until 1905 was consistently high among the batsmen. His best year with the bat was 1903, when he helped to win the championship. In eight games he scored 371 with an average of 41, and he also took 26 wickets at 17.23 to finish at the top of the bowlers, fractionally ahead of Hearne.

Bosanquet was among the most exciting cricketers of the time, a dashing batsman and a spin bowler who gave England victory in his first Test against Australia in 1905 by taking eight wickets for 107. He began bowling at medium pace and was then attracted by the current craze for leg spin. He was the man who discovered the googly, which was as commonly called a bosie. If he was always an erratic slow bowler, more so than most of his type, he could be very dangerous.

The googly was adopted most zealously in South Africa, and in 1907 four bowlers of that type carried all before them on tour in England. Schwarz, Vogler, Faulkner and White took 376 wickets at the low average cost of 14.13. They so dominated their team's work in the field that Kotze, the fast bowler, and the giant Sinclair, who had together taken more than 200 wickets on tour three years earlier, had little to do. They bowled only enough to take 63 wickets. Schwarz concentrated entirely on the googly, lest mixing it with the leg-break might cost him his accuracy. The other three used it in support of the leg break, which was their stock ball. Middlesex were one of the sides to suffer from the discovery made by their own Bosanquet while being beaten by 278 runs.

It was in 1900 that Bosanquet put himself in the front rank of

English cricketers by scoring a century in each innings against Leicestershire. In the next nine seasons he scored over 6,500 runs, averaging nearly 36, and took 265 wickets. They cost nearly 27 runs each, for there were times when his bowling was wild and costly. After that he played only two more county games before the war and six immediately after it.

J. W. Hearne and Patsy Hendren were playing for the county during the last half-dozen years before the war. Hendren, born in 1889, was two years the senior. He was in the championship side first, but Hearne rapidly overtook and passed him. In 1906 Hendren, whose elder brother Denis was already being tried in first-class cricket but who did not quite make the grade, was opening the innings for the second XI. He scored 76 against Kent's second XI. A year later Hearne played for the same side. He went in at number nine against Kent's second XI and bagged a pair. Against Sussex's second he was number 11, scoring three and two, and in the two matches he took two wickets for 132. In 1908 Hendren played for the first team but made only 76 in ten completed innings. At the next attempt his total was 698, which made his average over 19. He was also doing a little bowling at that time, but his five wickets in two seasons were costly, and from then onwards he was played for his batting and fielding. Hearne's first-team start in 1909 was modest, 130 runs at 11.8 and ten wickets for 186.

After that Hearne utterly outpaced Hendren. In 1910 he hit two centuries, 155 against Somerset and 108 against Sussex, and his total for the county was 725, which he supported by taking 48 wickets. A year later he doubled his tally of hundreds and almost doubled his runs and wickets. In the last two years before the war Middlesex had in Tarrant and Hearne two all-rounders who were almost a cricket side in themselves. Middlesex played only 22 matches, but together in 1913 they accounted for nearly 3,000 runs and took 223 wickets in those games.

The last pre-war season was one long triumphant procession for them. In their 22 matches Hearne topped 2,000 with an average of 74.85, and in second place Tarrant averaged 51 with an aggregate of 1,743. They also took the top two places among the bowlers. In this branch Tarrant was ahead, 131 wickets at 18.4, while Hearne followed with 114 at 21.4. They seemed to hunt as a pair. When Tarrant made 250 not out and 200 in successive innings against Essex and Worcestershire, Hearne' scores were 106 not out and 104, and together they had partnerships of 229 without being parted and 216. Shortly before they had put on 237 for the first wicket, Hearne 228 and Tarrant 77, while playing for M C C against the minor counties. They also made 380 for the second wicket against Lancashire, with Hearne 204 and Tarrant 198.

Hearne was a beautifully smooth and elegant batsman, so correct as to become unobtrusively part of the scenery. His stroke play was so effortless that his scoring-rate was faster than it appeared to be. He and Tarrant made their 380, which remains the best second-wicket stand for Middlesex, at almost 85 an hour. Hearne was only 20 went he was sent to Australia with Warner's M C C team in 1911. In his second Test, when his twenty-first birthday still lay ahead, he made a century. Subsequently, however, his Test record was singularly disappointing for such a highly gifted player, though indifferent health was one obvious reason. He had 24 Tests between 1911 and 1926, but his runs numbered only 806, and his leg break bowling brought only 30 wickets. His batting average was 26 and his bowling nearly 49. In fact he was active in only 23 Tests. His last was the first of the 1926 series at Trent Bridge, where he and eight other Englishmen never actually took the field. The weather allowed play sufficient only for Hobbs and Sutcliffe to make 32 without being parted.

Nevertheless Hearne's place among the great players is secure. He scored 37,252 runs with 96 centuries, averaging more than 40, and took 1,839 wickets. In both the last two pre-war years, and again in 1920, he exceeded 2,000 runs and 100 wickets in all first-class cricket.

The third of the Hearnes, who were cousins, and Hendren have always been closely associated, as subsequently Compton and Edrich were. There was not as much difference between Compton and Edrich as between Hearne and Hendren. The latter pair were utterly different both as men and as cricketers. Hearne, slightly built, was serious and quiet, so modestly retiring as to be almost remote. Hendren bubbled with zest of living. He was cut out to become a public character. Cricket was fortunate that it happened to be the direction he took. He was a short but roundly stocky man. His puckish face was a creation of generous curves with eyes always smiling and reflecting his infectious sense of fun. He was a humorist with a wealth of amusing stories, most of them culled from his own experiences. He was a leg-puller, but a kindly one. Indeed kind is the adjective most appropriate to the man. His most obvious characteristic was the friendliness which made him instantly and warmly accepted by all manner of people as one of themselves. There has surely been no more lovable character in sport. As Ian Peebles wrote: ' Some famous players achieve public acclaim and popularity by their play while evoking no great feeling of affection among those close to them.' That Hendren was as well liked – indeed loved is hardly too strong a word – by his fellow-players as by the public indicates his stature.

Patsy was not one to be taken too literally. His tongue was often in his cheek. Alf Gover tells a story against himself, in which Hendren was the spoofer. Gover was then a very young man in the Surrey side. When he went to play a county match at Lord's for the first time, he arrived at the ground long before the other Surrey players. The professionals then had their own dressing-rooms in the small pavilion to the north of the main pavilion. Only Hendren was there when Gover arrived. He welcomed the youngster, asked his name and what he did as a cricketer. Gover admitted to being a fast bowler.

' Very fast?' asked Hendren, his eyes popping and a look of apprehension on his face.

' Oh yes,' said Gover.

' Well don't forget I'm an old man. When I come in, don't drop them short.'

Gover duly took the wicket which brought Hendren to the middle. He had three balls to go in the over, and he fancied his chances of another wicket against the man who did not care for fast bowling pitched short. Gover bowled short, and from Hendren's bat the ball cannoned into the square-leg boundary pickets in front of the Tavern. Muttering ' bloody fluke' to himself as he walked back to his mark, the fast bowler wound himself up to put still more into his next short one. The result was more disastrous, the ball carrying into the crowd over the Tavern boundary for six. Still not persuaded, Gover bowled a third short one which produced another four hooked in the same direction.

As the fielders crossed over Jack Hobbs walked over to ask Gover why he was bowling short to Patsy.

'He doesn't like them,' replied Gover.

'Who told you that?'

'He told me so himself.'

Hobbs laughed and said: 'Don't you know he's an Irishman and kisses the blarney stone before each season? Don't ever bowl short at him again. He's the best hooker in the game.'

Hendren was not least loved in the West Indies, where he played up to the excited participation of spectators in the play. Patsy to the public generally, Pat to his team mates and 'Spud' to Jack Hearne, to whom he was so close, he was universally the darling of the game. Everywhere his appearance on the ground evoked in the words of Peebles 'a spontaneous demonstration of joy. The Hill at Sydney, or the stately tents at Canterbury, would greet him in rather different terms, but with the same warmth.'

His cricket reflected his personality. It bubbled with enjoyment. He was nimble on his feet, he was master of stroke play, and, in particular, of that famous hook, the off drive and the cut. In the field he was one of the great outfields. His point of balance enabled him, like his successor Sid Brown, to pick up the ball at full speed. He was no less expert near the wicket.

In the years before the First World War his progress was much less spectacular than Hearne's. He lifted his average well up into the 30s, but he only once exceeded 1,000 runs in championship games. It was in the post-war period that he came to greatness. His only serious setback then was suffered in 1921, the year in which Australia's fast bowlers Gregory and Macdonald, were invincible. In the first two Tests he made four low scores and did not play for England again that summer. Yet he came bounding back, and his Test career did not end until 1934. At the age of 45 he then scored at Old Trafford the last of his seven centuries for England when he, Sutcliffe and Leyland rallied the side after Bill O'Reilly had taken three wickets in four balls. By then he had played 51 matches and averaged 47.6 with a grand total of 3,525 and a top score of 205 not out.

Two other professionals came to the front in this time. H. R. Murrell, who first played for Kent, was the admirable successor behind the stumps to MacGregor, but he was playing in the side very usefully as a sound batsman before the changeover took place and keeping when MacGregor could not play, which was not infrequent. Harry Lee first played in 1911 as an all-rounder. In 1914 he began going in first, where he had much success subsequently, and in that season as Tarrant's partner he made his first century, 139 against Nottinghamshire at Lord's.

The professionals had taken on the main burden, but the flow of good amateurs into the side continued. In the last years of the century Stoddart, O'Brien and Ford were the leading batsmen, with J. T. Hearne taking the wickets. O'Brien remained at the top in the first two seasons of the new championship, averaging with Stoddart just over 40. In 1897 his average was halved, and the next year he retired. Stoddart continued into the new century, but only just. He dropped out of the game when still full of cricket. He had a particularly good summer in 1898, when he returned after a surprisingly indifferent season in Australia. He topped 1,000 and averaged 52.89. Ford also exceeded 1,000, but his average was 12 fewer. Stoddart was expected to succeed Webbe as captain. Instead he played only one game in the next season, in which he made a duck, and the captaincy passed to MacGregor. The reason put out at the time was that he was tired of playing, but *Wisden* poured scorn on the suggestion.

Stoddart did come back briefly for Hearne's Benefit in 1900. He played one match against Sussex to get the feel of things again but scored only a single. In the Benefit match against Somerset he was again out cheaply for 12, but in the second innings he batted for nearly five hours and made 221, the highest score of his first-class career.

The year 1900 was also Webbe's last. In latter years he had continued to score usefully, with an average in the middle 20s, and to give the innings ballast. In his only game he finished his career for the county by scoring 59 not out and helping W. P. Robertson in a long stand which saved the game against Somerset. Ford had played his final game the previous summer. He did not intend to retire, but illness kept him out of the game in 1900, and he never reappeared.

It was as well for Middlesex that the supply of first-class amateurs was particularly good at that time. Bosanquet, Warner, Wells, James Douglas, the most successful of four brothers who played for the county, George Beldam, Robertson and H. B. Hayman were there to carry on with the new skipper. MacGregor had played his eight Tests against Australia in the nineties. His keeping was now said to be falling off, but he more than held his own for several more years.

Douglas and his brother, R. N., were, like Wells, schoolmasters available only towards the end of the season, when they appreciably lifted the fielding standard. Fielding comparisons between different periods are perhaps more difficult to make than those of batting and bowling. It is, however, quite obvious that the catching at that time could not have approached the present standard. The new century was not far advanced when Sydney Pardon commented on the number of catches dropped. In the week of the Gentlemen *v* Players match alone there were 53 straightforward misses, a figure which excluded the half-chances, so many of which are picked up in the close-catching positions now.

In the period from 1896 to 1908 there was no steadier or more reliable scorer than James Douglas, particularly on soft pitches. In those years his average only once dropped below 30, and that fractionally. Several times it was above 40, and when all the other batsmen had an off-season in 1902, Warner, Bosanquet and Trott among them, he finished all alone at the top of the list with 474 runs at almost 40 an innings. His usual ration of games was eight to nine. His longest season was in 1901, when he played 11 times and scored 746. His brother, R. N., had his best season three years earlier with an average of 32.

Hayman and Dr G. Thornton, who often scored well in the late nineties, came from the same stable as Stoddart. Among the clubs Hampstead were indeed almost as valuable to the county as Southgate, which had supplied the Walkers. Hayman was a 30-an-innings man, and even more valuable was George Beldam, who added wickets to the many runs he made.

The universities were naturally the source of many acquisitions. Oxford had given them Webbe, O'Brien and, later, Bosanquet and Warner. Cambridge in the nineties served the county very well indeed: in 1890, when the university made 703 for nine against Sussex, the first four batsmen were Middlesex players, and their scoring was remarkable. Three were century-makers, C. P. Foley with 117, Francis Ford with 191 and Mac-Gregor with 131. The other, R. N. Douglas, made 62. The fifth batsman was Stanley Jackson with 60, and Ford's fourth-wicket partnership with him brought 132 in 65 minutes. Two years later James Douglas joined his brother in the University side, and together they opened the innings. Meanwhile C. M. Wells had also arrived in the Cambridge team. L. J. Moon, who, playing a few matches each season, was to make more than 2,000 runs for Middlesex, was another Blue of the nineties. Early in the new century other similarly valuable county players from Cambridge were W. P. Robertson, M. W. Payne and C. C. Page. Despite Warner and Bosanquet, the gains from Oxford in the same period were not as great, though R. E. More and W. S. Bird were useful occasional players. Robertson had made 118 against Worcestershire in Webbe's last match during the year before that in which he won his Blue at Cambridge. On that occasion Middlesex lost six wickets for 75 and were plunging to defeat, when he joined Webbe in a stand of 167. Robertson was still serving Middlesex well in 1914, when he hit a century against Nottinghamshire and made 580 runs with an average of 38.6. He also played with some success immediately after the War. Several amateurs who were to do more in the following period, started playing towards the end of the Golden Age. The Hon C. N. Bruce first represented the county in 1908 but played little before the war. Frank Mann began a year later and was followed at intervals by E. L. Kidd, Sammy Saville, Dick Twining, Gerald Crutchley and Nigel Haig. Saville was one of the greatest hockey players, and, as becomes an inside-forward in that fastest of field games, he was a brilliant fielder anywhere on the off side, the main target of stroke-play at the time. Two other amateurs, the brothers Littel-john, were distinguished players in those years, when they could be available. In 1911 A. R. Litteljohn, leaving Tarrant and the two Hearnes in his wake, bowled himself to the top of the averages with 46 wickets at 16.95. A year later his brother, E. S., headed the batsmen with 43.3 from 389 runs. That was an exceptional performance in an unusually wet summer, with so many treacherous pitches that the average of Warner, who was second, was only 33.6.

So to Plum Warner with his picturesque Harlequin cap, who, over a long period, did as much for Middlesex cricket as the Walkers and Webbe. From the time he first won his Blue at Oxford in 1895 until long after the Second World War his energies were devoted to cricket, and particularly that of Middle-sex and Lord's, where many of his greatest innings were played. His bad health was a handicap. Several times illness caused him to drop out of the county side in the early years of this century. Then in 1911, when he was captain of the M C C touring team in Australia for the second time, another breakdown turned him into a non-combatant. Johnny Douglas took over the leadership and enjoyed the triumph which the great bowling of Sidney Barnes and Frank Foster achieved.

Yet Warner's batting success was consistent. He made his first century for the county in 1899 against Yorkshire. The timing of that innings is interesting. He spent 140 minutes over the first 50, 100 minutes over the second, and finally knocked up the last 50 in an hour. His soundness, matched by determination, made Warner the batsman. In 1900 he exceeded 1,000 for the first time, in spite of a bout of illness, and between then and his retirement, after winning the championship in 1920, he made more than 16,000 runs for Middlesex alone and averaged close to 40. He played in 15 Tests and represented the Gentlemen against the Players 14 times. In all first-class cricket he scored 60 centuries.

His record, for a man of frail physique and indifferent health during many of his playing years, who played for a county side with fewer matches each season than the other leading counties, was good enough. Yet his value as captain and later as elder statesman surely meant even more to Middlesex. For some years before he became the official captain in 1908 he was MacGregor's deputy. He was, therefore, quite an experienced leader when he took the M C C team to Australia in 1903. Warner was the quiet gentle-mannered type of skipper, who had no need to drive his men to get the best out of them. He was one under whom they liked playing, and inevitably they played their hardest for him. His own cricket set an example of grit and determination, and he was an optimist who could visualise eventual victory in the most forbidding circumstances. That quality must have had much to do with the remarkable defeat of Surrey in the final match of the 1920 campaign, which enabled them to snatch the championship.

Middlesex have generally been fortunate in their skippers, and never more so than in their first 50 years. To have five such captains as V. E. and I. D. Walker, Webbe, MacGregor and Warner was richness indeed. The Walkers' association with the club extended from the formation in 1864 until R. D. died in 1922. He succeeded V. E. as President in 1906 and so was the figurehead when Warner landed his championship. I. D. died in July 1898, and the county match with Kent was postponed until August to allow the team to go to his funeral.

MacGregor is one of the few who have made a success of the dual roles of skipper and wicket-keeper. It is the most difficult position from which to lead a side, for wicket-keeping itself demands the player's entire concentration. Nevertheless MacGregor was an admirable captain from 1899 until 1907, though in that time he missed some matches each year. He has strong claims to be regarded as England's best amateur wicket-keeper of all time. He excelled at taking fast bowling standing close up to the wicket, not least when he was in the Cambridge side. There he kept to the fiery fast bowling of Sammy Woods, the Australian who played Test cricket both for Australia and England.

While MacGregor and Warner were the captains, two players who afterwards went to South Africa and gained considerable distinction for that country played in first-class company for the first time in the county side. Schwarz played in 1901, when he made 171 in three innings, one of which was unfinished, and 1902, when he played 11 matches but averaged only 9.16.

Schwarz had not yet developed his googly bowling, and in those years he managed only one wicket for 117. When he later played a single county match as a bowler he took six wickets for 67. The other was M. J. Susskind. He did little for Middlesex, and it was not until the mid-twenties that he batted with success in Test cricket. So, with Vogler and Halliwell, Middlesex had four South African international players in their ranks. Between the wars Owen-Smith made the total five.

Between 1895 and 1914 a dozen professionals, one or two of whom appeared on the scene only fleetingly, and more than 100 amateurs played. Not all who made valuable contributions have yet had mention, batsmen such as the Hon R. Anson, who was more prominent after the war, M. H. C. Doll, G. F. S. Griffin and G. L. Hebden, and a bowler in G. G. Napier. And in 1912 one of the many Foster brothers, who caused Worcestershire at that time to be familiarly known as Fostershire, played 11 matches for them. He was Basil, who became more famous as an actor.

3 Ups and Downs, 1895-1914

The modern period started in 1895 with Middlesex finishing equal seventh with Warwickshire. They played Essex and the other eight counties who had been ranked with them as first-class before the championship was reformed, giving them 18 matches. Essex appeared on their list only because they needed two more matches to qualify for the competition. The next year Middlesex reverted to the original eight. Their results at this time were, accordingly, not helped by matches against the weaker counties.

Until that year only Webbe and Stoddart had exceeded 200 in an innings. Stoddart was also the only Middlesex batsman to score a century in each innings, which he did at Lord's in 1893 against Nottinghamshire. O'Brien now hit their second double century, 202 against Sussex. J. T. Hearne took 105 wickets in the 18 championship matches, and he continued to reel off the hundreds when they were down to 16 matches. Ford played only once that summer, but the side was reinforced by Wells, who had previously played for Surrey, the champions that year.

Middlesex rose to third place in 1896 and had two games of vastly differing fortune against Surrey. On both occasions the pitch was the deciding factor. At the Oval, Surrey batted twice on pitches affected by rain and were defeated by 205 runs. O'Brien played a great innings of 137, under conditions not by any means in his favour, and Hearne and Rawlin bowled unchanged to rout Surrey twice. Hearne took six wickets for 26 and six for 64, and Rawlin had four wickets for 15 and four for 54. Rawlin was not so well in the picture when he took his Benefit against Somerset. He made a duck, and, while Hearne was taking 12 wickets and giving Middlesex an innings win, he failed to take one. The return with Surrey at Lord's went quite the other way. The dry pitch was beginning to break up even before Surrey completed their innings of 300. It became progressively worse while Middlesex were struggling to 159 and 83. They were beaten by the fast bowling of Tom Richardson, who took five in each innings. Both O'Brien and Stoddart averaged above 40 that season, and the latter made three centuries. James Douglas also had an excellent season. He lifted his average to 30, and in one great fortnight he shared with Stoddart opening stands of 178 against Yorkshire, 158 against Nottinghamshire and 166 against Kent.

From third they dropped promptly to equal seventh, and again they were bracketed with Warwickshire. O'Brien slipped back, and Stoddart was out for much of the season nursing a knee injury, though he batted as well as ever when he did play. Francis Ford, however, played more often than in the preceding seasons and, with a top score of 150 against Gloucestershire, he had an average of 40. So did James Douglas. The batting indeed was satisfactory, and the reason for the fall in the championship was the lack of strong bowling support for Hearne until Wells joined the team late in the season. Rawlin was now aged 40, and his best bowling days were behind him. His 52 wickets cost over 25, which was expensive by current standards.

Throughout this period Middlesex rose as quickly as they descended. They were a resilient side, and now they were powerfully reinforced by Trott. In his first season he and Hearne each took more than 100 wickets, and they jumped to second place behind Yorkshire. This year they had 18 matches and won ten of them. Their games with Yorkshire followed much the same course as those with Surrey two years earlier. Yorkshire won the first at Lord's by an innings and nine runs, despite Ford's hitting 127 out of 170 inside two hours of glorious attacking cricket. The return was played at Leeds in rainy conditions, which might have been thought more favourable to Yorkshire. It did not turn out that way. The scores were Yorkshire 142 and 45, Middlesex 128 and 62 for two wickets – victory for the latter by eight wickets. On the second day 15 wickets fell for 65 before lunch, the last five of Middlesex and all ten of Yorkshire in the second innings. Trott was irresistible and outshone Hearne on this occasion. He had four wickets for 70 in the first innings and then seven for 13 in 14.1 overs. Hearne's total share was six wickets for 73.

Trott missed the first four games after injuring his hand in a match before the county season began. He had ample time to do so, for the first match was not played until the end of May. The batting excellently supported the work of the two great bowlers. Stoddart averaged 52, both Ford and Douglas exceeded 40, and Wells 38. Moreover Warner was so consistent that, although his top score was no more than 88, he averaged almost 34, and the other Douglas, R. N., was close behind.

They were again second in 1899, and by any points-scoring system in use from 1920 onwards – excluding perhaps the odd methods based on first-innings bonus points of recent years – they would have been champions. Surrey won ten, lost two and drew 14. Middlesex won 11, lost three and drew four. At the time, however, drawn games were ignored. One point was given for each win, and a point was deducted for each defeat. The order in the championship was decided by the proportionate number of points in finished matches. In that year, therefore, the fact that Surrey won only ten of 26 matches while Middlesex had 11 wins in 16 meant nothing. Surrey had eight points out of a possible 12, proportionately better than the eight points of Middlesex out of a possible 14. In 1910 the method was changed so that the championship was decided by the proportionate number of points in all games. In 1911 it was changed again to five points for a win and three for first-innings lead and one for the side behind in a drawn match. The order was decided by the percentage of points to the maximum possible. After the First World War the changes became more frequent, and the logic behind them was not always clear.

That was the first of Trott's two golden seasons. He played an outstanding innings against Yorkshire of 164. After a careful start he slammed the last 137 out of 181 in 90 minutes. This was also the year of Rawlin's only century, which contributed to the win over Surrey at Lord's. In their other match, an innings of 147 by Ford deprived Surrey of victory. Another outstanding performance was the all-round success of Wells against Nottinghamshire. He made 244, batting for five hours and three-quarters, and in the two innings he took nine wickets for 111 runs.

Their major failure that year was in the match with the Australians -- defeat by the overwhelming margin of an innings and 230 runs. Joe Darling and Frank Iredale each scored 111 and shared a long and sedate partnership, which caused some barracking among the spectators. It sounds mild enough in the light of the barracking which has sometimes erupted into ugly scenes and even rioting in more recent years. At the time to *Wisden*, recording the game, it seemed sacrilege! 'On the first day the game was marred by an unseemly demonstration on the part of the spectators, happily without precedent at Lord's ground.' It seems that the extreme caution of Darling and Iredale was accompanied by ironical cheering when a run was scored, and spectators whistled the 'Dead March in Saul'. How spectators must have changed! There would be very few able to take up the dirge today, if anybody was able to start whistling it!

However cautious they may have been, the batting of Darling and Iredale had the desired outcome. Middlesex were out for 105 and 110, routed by McLeod and Jones. Jones, the fast bowler who once shocked W. G. Grace by sending a ball through his luxuriant beard, was one of those accused at that time of chucking. The trouble came to a head in the following year, and the bowlers most immediately concerned were Mold of Lancashire and Tyler of Somerset, a slow bowler. Umpire Phillips, who stood in matches both in England and Australia, took the part played in modern cricket by Sid Buller and no-balled Mold repeatedly for throwing. As in Buller's case years later, Phillips came in for much ill-judged abuse, but his correct action had its effect. The problem was tackled, primarily by the county captains' agreeing to stamp out the evil, and the law-makers at Lord's were not required to take official action.

Though Middlesex slipped to equal seventh with Gloucestershire and Surrey in 1900, they did the double against Surrey for the first time since 1893. Whereas the previous summer they had won their first six matches outright they now had a bad start. At the end of June they had won only one match out of nine, for Hearne and Trott were not on their best form. From that point, however, they carried all before them. Trott took 154 of his 211 wickets for Middlesex and Hearne 95. The only win during the first half of the season was in Hearne's Benefit match, in which Stoddart made his final 221. On the Somerset side Tyler, the suspect bowler, took seven wickets for 60 runs in the first innings.

Though Warner was again upset by illness he had a notable season with five centuries, a total of 1,335 runs and an average of almost 45. Warner, who played fast bowling especially well, had arrived. George Beldam started in county cricket, followed three years later by his brother, E. A. After the Cambridge term Robertson made more than 500 runs, and Bosanquet established his class by scoring a century in each innings against Leicestershire. That set them on the way to winning eight of their last 13 matches – they played 22 that year.

Hearne was at his best against Surrey, and took 16 wickets in the two games. Moreover, in the first of them at the Oval he arrived at the wicket when Middlesex had lost nine second-innings wickets and still needed 18. These were slowly collected by W. Williams, an amateur batting at number ten, and Hearne, defying Lockwood's best fast bowling. In the return Warner scored a century, as did Bobby Abel for Surrey, and Trott and Hearne skittled the foe for 64 in the second innings.

Twice that season the strong Middlesex bowling was collared and hammered by two of the most brilliant amateurs of the age. In the middle of June Gilbert Jessop, the most renowned of all smiters, came to Lord's in the Gloucestershire side and cut loose. In his first half-hour he reached 50 out of 57, was 101 half an hour later, and finally, when bowled by Roche, he had walloped 109 out of 120 in only 67 minutes. Six weeks later they suffered the full range of Ranjitsinhji's glorious stroke play at Hove. Though a worn pitch was helping the bowlers, Ranji hit 35 fours and in three hours made 202. With C. Aubrey Smith, who later became famous as a film star in Hollywood, he put on 88 for the eighth wicket in 35 minutes, and Smith's share was two.

The next season Middlesex bounded up the table as rapidly as they had decended it. They were second once again in 1901, when Yorkshire were the champions. They lost only twice and won six matches, but, with Hearne having an off-season in championship games, and the averages of most others being somewhat high, ten were left drawn. The strength lay in the batting. Ten different batsmen scored centuries. Warner had three, Bosanquet and James Douglas two each, and H. B. Chinnery, Hayman, Moon, More, Robertson, Trott and Wells made one each. Chinnery's complete career with Middlesex amounted to only seven innings. Trott's century, 112 against Essex, was made in the last match, and it was almost the only innings in which he batted really well. Warner with 1,381 championship runs improved his average to 49.33, Bosanquet passed 1,000, James Douglas had 746, Wells, George Beldam, Moon, Hayman, Robertson, More and R. N. Douglas scored usefully, and the side was seldom short of runs.

The best bowling average, however, was Trott's 23.57 from 89 wickets. Wells took 39, but they cost almost 25 each, and Hearne had such an indifferent championship season that his average climbed to 30.9. Bosanquet sometimes bowled at his original medium pace and sometimes used leg breaks. He had not yet mastered them, nor unearthed the googly. His 34 wickets cost nearly 35 runs each. Both matches with Surrey were drawn. In the second, at the Oval, Abel made 205 and batted more than five hours. Surrey's total was 559 for eight wickets declared, and the Middlesex bowling makes sorry reading with one somewhat unexpected exception. The veteran Rawlin, whose bag in that championship campaign was only 23 wickets, took five for 88. The others who toiled, largely in vain, were Trott with no wicket for 117, Wells with one for 61, J. Douglas with none for 20, More with none for 92, Bosanquet with two for 79 and Hearne with none for 70. Hearne had temporarily lost his snap, but he remained as steady as ever, and those 70 came slowly off 32 overs. In the previous year the over had been increased from five balls to six.

Once more the county was to drop suddenly, for a year later they had slipped from second to twelfth position. They lost twice to Surrey, for whom Abel made yet another century, and they won only three games. Again in a wet summer the bowling generally was weak, and only James Douglas had any reason to be pleased with his batting. Warner was down to an average of

27.5, and even that was success by comparison with Bosanquet's 16.4. Hearne did improve on his previous summer's record, as well he might on pitches often affected by rain, and he did the hat-trick, when he and Trott bowled Essex out for 64 on a sticky wicket at Lord's. There had been no play on the first two days, and, though 24 wickets fell on the third, the match was drawn. MacGregor had an outstanding wicket-keeping day at Nottingham. In the Notts second innings he stumped five batsmen, including Shrewsbury and William Gunn, four off Bosanquet and the other off Wells.

Having failed so disappointingly in one wet season, their success during another damp one in 1903 was remarkable. With much the same side, playing in much the same conditions, they jumped to top place. They won eight times and lost only once in 16 games; and they confirmed their right to the title by their play against powerful opposition in the Champion County *v* The Rest of England match at the Oval. Hearne returned to form, and all the bowling figures were vastly improved, Bosanquet cutting 17 off his average. The batsmen, too, redeemed their failures of the previous summer. Beldam led them with 854 runs in 13 matches, Warner and Bosanquet were back to form, and Moon, who had not played in the previous year, returned to hit two centuries. The one man who did comparatively little was the 1902 success, Douglas. He made his highest score, 204, against Gloucestershire, but his other 13 innings produced only 207.

Middlesex were not defeated until the second week in August. Yorkshire, the runners-up, trounced them by 230 runs after Hirst and Rhodes had routed them for 79 in the first innings without any important help from the pitch. That set-back might have shaken them, but the weather made sure that their hold on the top position was not shaken. A series of draws followed, which could not influence the championship scoring. Day after day was ruined by the weather, and the match with Kent at Lord's was a total wash-out. It was not until the final match, against Surrey, that another definite result could be reached. Middlesex were in top gear and won by an innings. A century by George Beldam, his second against Surrey that season, retrieved a poor batting start, and, when Hearne and Trott had Surrey batting after rain,

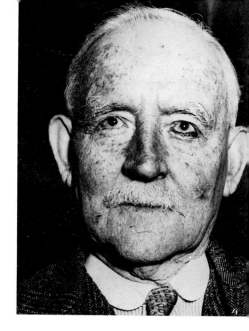

Right, A. J. Webbe, one of the earliest Middlesex captains
Below, J. T. Hearne, three years after his last county match, but still playing and coaching at Eton
Below right, Albert Trott, the first of the county's great modern all-rounders and first of their Australian imports

Left, Frank Tarrant, also from Australia and an even finer all-rounder than Trott
Above, Plum Warner, perhaps the best Middlesex captain, who led the county to
their third championship in his last season. Here he goes to bat at the Oval in the
Champion County *v* The Rest match

J. W. Hearne, Young Jack, leg break bowler and one of the game's most elegantly correct batsmen
Below, Patsy Hendren, batting against Surrey, with W. J. Abel fielding in the gully, playing one of his famous hooks

they were helpless. Hearne had four wickets for 26, Trott six for 19, and Surrey, skittled in 24.4 overs for 57, had to follow on 224 behind. They managed only 130, Wells this time taking the leading bowling part with five for 26. Bobby Abel was no longer in the Surrey side to torment them, and they won the first encounter at Lord's also. Beldam, coming straight from success at Lord's, where he made 80 and 54 for the Gentlemen against the Players, scored 89 and 118. Bosanquet made 52 and 97 and finished the match by taking six wickets for 46 to give Middlesex a winning margin of 221 runs. In the first ten years of the new championship Middlesex had the better of the exchanges, for they again won both games in 1904 and had then won nine to Surrey's six, with five left drawn.

In the middle of September they returned to the Oval to have rather the better of their match with The Rest. Beldam was again in great form, with his scores of 57 and 88 not out; Warner made a century, and at the close, after Middlesex had declared their second innings, The Rest at 229 for five wickets were still 71 behind. The position was actually more favourable to the county than the figures suggest. They led by 46 on the first innings, and after Warner and Beldam had put on 158 for their second wicket the following batsmen sacrificed themselves while slamming the score to declaration point at 254 for eight. Even an innings of 76 in 70 minutes by Hirst could not hold out hope of victory to The Rest.

Middlesex again did well in 1904 and finished fourth. They also had an epic tie-match with the South Africans, in which Bosanquet scored 110 and 44. Their finest achievement was to defeat Surrey by two wickets at Lord's in a match of modest scoring. They were headed on the first innings by 70, and, after Ernie Hayes had scored his second 50 for Surrey, they were set a target of 250. Jack Crawford then bowled at speed so well that Warner, James Douglas, E. Field and Bosanquet were soon out for 21. George Beldam batted for four hours and played one of his finest innings for 98. He then added 88 with Wells, and with Beldam and MacGregor 80. Yet, with eight wickets down, 54 runs were still needed. For once Trott resisted the temptation to indulge in heroics, and he made 23 while helping MacGregor carry the side to victory. MacGregor's 63 not out was his highest score of the year.

Bosanquet, who had a great season and took more than 50 wickets in August, had one wicket for 2 and six for 75 in that match. Immediately afterwards, when Middlesex had an even more exciting win by one wicket against Kent, he had three for 76 and five for 23. Middlesex on that occasion had to score 135 against the left-arm bowling of Colin Blythe on a rain-marred pitch. Blythe duly took five wickets, and Kent seemed to have the game safe when the eighth wicket fell at 90. Wells and M. W. Payne, however, added 45, enjoying the luck against Blythe, and the scores were level at the fall of the ninth wicket. Hearne was the number 11 and played through the rest of the over from fast bowler Fielder. Off the third ball of the next over, bowled by J. R. Mason, Wells made the winning run.

Bosanquet also had an outstanding batting season, passing 1,000 and taking the leading place with a championship average of 41.6. Warner, Douglas and Beldam were also consistent scorers, and Beldam had the pleasing experience of sharing a stand of 201 in only two hours for the fifth wicket against Somerset at Lord's with his brother, E. A. Each brother scored a century. That match was also a triumph for Hearne, who headed the bowling averages. In the first innings he took eight wickets for 49 and, in the second, seven for 44.

There were some curious individual failures and successes that summer. K. I. Nicholl, an Etonian, played in two matches and had three innings, all of which brought him dismissal for ducks. R. W. Nicholls started the season with four ducks and ended it by bagging a pair. His average from eight matches was 5.36. Trott also had a long run of failures with nine scores below ten in succession. More satisfying was the experience of More, who returned from a spell abroad. Against Yorkshire at Sheffield he went in at number 10 and made 120 not out in 100 minutes. He and Bosanquet, whose score was 141, added 128 in 48 minutes, and with Hearne he put on 91 for the last wicket in 52 minutes. Though Hearne generally batted last, he had a lofty place in the championship averages with 32.28 and a total of 226. He was not out 18 times – eight in his first nine and again eight in his last nine innings.

Middlesex were due for another lapse – and it came. They plunged to eleventh place in the table. The reasons were numerous. Not least was the low standard of the fielding, 'deplorably bad' in August according to *Wisden*. Three amateurs, who made hundreds, Field, Page and J. H. Stogden, could play little. That was also the case with Moon and J. H. Hunt, an all-rounder. Trott was slipping back fast, as his championship averages indicate: 14.5 with the bat and almost 29 with the ball. George Beldam appeared in only eight matches, and those without much success. Hearne's bowling results were fair, but the wickets of most bowlers that season were generally costly.

The arrival of Tarrant and Mignon did not immediately make good the deficiences. Tarrant's first season was quite ordinary, and Mignon's nine wickets were expensive. If Bosanquet's bowling was not so successful, he had another fine batting season. He had three centuries, two of them in the match against Sussex at Lord's, and both he and Douglas averaged more than 40. Warner, having just before scored 204 for M C C against Sussex, began the championship season with a pair against Gloucestershire, but overall his scoring was as regular as ever.

Tarrant played one significant innings, which foreshadowed his future success, when he batted four hours and a half for 162 not out at Leyton. On the same occasion Hearne made his highest score. He had taken eight wickets for 93 in an Essex total of 268, and now he and Tarrant shared an unfinished ninth-wicket stand of 98. Hearne's share was 56.

Honours were even in the matches with Surrey. Middlesex won at Lord's thanks largely to a century by Douglas. At the Oval none of the first three innings reached 150. The fiery fast bowling of Neville Knox, four wickets for 74 and eight for 48, was too much for Middlesex, and on the other side Mignon had his solitary success in eight matches by taking seven for 63. Finally Surrey had to make 167. The pitch had been difficult, but it played better in the final innings, and Surrey hit off the runs without loss. The batting partners were Tom Hayward and Jack Hobbs, who was in his first season and forming the first of his great opening partnerships – Hayward and Hobbs, Hobbs and Rhodes, Hobbs and Sandham and, greatest of all, Hobbs and Sutcliffe.

This time Middlesex did not immediately spring up the table from a lowly position. Although Tarrant fully found his niche in county cricket, they were again eleventh in 1906. Warner was the only amateur regularly available. Bosanquet played only three matches, sufficient for him to make one of the only four centuries scored for the county, and he could spare little time for first-class cricket in subsequent seasons. Warner scored two of the other centuries and Tarrant one. In 19 matches no fewer than 37 players were used, including an unfortunate amateur, L. G. Colbeck, who had five ducks in succession. Tarrant was much the most successful bowler, 73 wickets for the county, and Mignon, 68 at 25.23, enjoyed the first of six good, but not startling seasons. Hearne, however, did so little for the county that his 34 wickets cost 30.8 each. He was at his lowest point. Warner, starting this time very differently with 137 against Sussex, and Tarrant were the main run getters.

There were more notable performances against than for Middlesex. They included a century by Hobbs at the Oval in the second innings to give Surrey a win. Hayward had scored a century in the first. Professional bowlers who were otherwise of no lasting fame prospered against Middlesex. At Hove, when Sussex beat them by an innings, E. B. Dwyer took 16 for 100 runs. A. E. Lewis of Somerset played a similar part in the overthrow of Middlesex with 11 for 103. A much more familiar name is Schofield Haigh, who took 12 wickets for 105 while Yorkshire were winning by 281 runs at Lord's. Middlesex won only five matches, but two of them were at the expense of Lancashire, who were to figure in an unpleasant incident at Lord's a year later in 1907. In the Lord's match this time Trott put in one of his now increasingly rare performances by taking five wickets for 46 in the second innings.

The Lancashire trouble occurred on the second day of the match. Rain had so marred the first day's play that only 25 overs were bowled, from which Lancashire made 57 for one wicket. The next day was fine, and spectators were admitted in anticipation of play. About 600 paid at the gate, but the ground was so saturated that no cricket was possible. When the day's play was called off, those who had paid gathered in front of the pavilion to demonstrate their annoyance. On the way across the ground some walked across the pitch, which was inspected by the captains after the crowd had dispersed.

In autocratic fashion, and with no regard for the regulations and ethics of the game, Lancashire's captain, Archie MacLaren, called the match off in its entirety. His pompous statement to the press read: 'Owing to the pitch having been deliberately torn up by the public, I, as captain of the Lancashire eleven cannot see my way to continue the game, the groundsman bearing me out that the wicket could not be again put right.'

Nobody else agreed with him. Those who saw the pitch next day said it had rolled out hard and true. His action was roundly condemned by critics and players including W. G. Grace writing in the *Morning Post*. Lancashire had abandoned the match without the agreement of MacGregor. Middlesex, however, did not claim the match, as was their right, and it was listed as drawn in the season's records.

From 1907 until the outbreak of war in 1914 Middlesex shed their habits of inconsistency. They were never out of the first six and ended the period as runner-up to Surrey. For most of that time Warner was the skipper, for after 1907 MacGregor retired. In his final season he had 34 victims and a batting average of 17 in 13 matches.

Increasing dependence on professionals regularly available largely accounts for the greater consistency. They finished the period with six: Tarrant, the two Hearnes, Murrell, Hendren and Lee. Warner was a seventh regular, with Mignon by that time in reserve. Warner had reached the peak of his skill. He was so splendidly consistent in 1907 that, although he had only one century, against Surrey at the Oval, his 1,353 runs gave him a county average of almost 45. A year later he had five centuries and an average of 54 in Middlesex matches. His batting matched the consistency of his side, and he maintained his form up to and including 1913. In the final season before the war his average slipped into the 20s for the first time since 1902.

Tarrant contributed greatly to the steady progress. In 1907 he first exceeded 1,000 runs and 100 wickets for Middlesex – to which he added materially in other first-class games – and he did so in most subsequent seasons. His totals in 1907 were 1,552 and 183 wickets at the splendidly low cost of 15.7. Trott had a revival in this, his Benefit year, when he had his two hat-tricks in the same innings. His total bag was 96 wickets at 16.67, and Hearne's average was little higher. Warner that year played his finest innings against Surrey at the Oval, where he scored a century before lunch, having hit his first 50 in only 45 minutes. Both Surrey matches produced tall scoring, with more than 1,200 runs on each occasion, and were left drawn. Warner's 149 was supported by 79 from James Douglas, and the opening stand brought 232 in two hours and a half. Surrey's retort was made strongly by Hayes who scored at 50 an hour while making 202 by powerful driving, which accounted for a high proportion of his 30 fours. He and Crawford, 82, added 183 in an hour and three-quarters, and with the skipper, Lord Dalmeny, who made 50, a stand of 84 was compressed into 27 minutes.

The match at Lord's belonged to Hayward and Hobbs. Earlier in the week they had had stands of 106 and 125 against Cambridge University. Against Middlesex their partnerships were 147 and 105. Middlesex themselves did some heavy scoring, and James Douglas shared three century-stands in the course of his 180 against Somerset at Taunton. He put on 110 for the first wicket with Warner, 103 for the second with H. A. Milton and 155 for the third with Tarrant, who went on to make 147. The total was 552, which followed 483 in the previous game at Bristol. In that game Tarrant took four wickets in four balls and altogether nine for 41 in Gloucestershire's second innings of 69.

Middlesex were themselves the victims of similar bowling at Sheffield. There Hirst's swing in a strong cross-wind was so devastating that he hit the stumps seven times and finished with nine wickets for 45, Middlesex being dismissed for 91. Hearne's best performance followed at Manchester. His five wickets for 38 and six for 29 brought about Lancashire's defeat by an innings. In the next match, at Trent Bridge, he had seven for 42 and three for 29, but Nottinghamshire still won by five wickets. Then it was Tarrant's turn again, at eight for 49, to snatch a remarkable victory from Sussex. The latter needed only 96 in the final innings but could manage only 84. In this low-scoring game

– top total 222 by Sussex – Murrell, playing as a batsman while M. W. Payne kept wicket in the absence of MacGregor, was the top Middlesex scorer with 63, in which were ten fours from front-foot driving.

The availability of Bosanquet for nine matches, after which he became virtually a stranger to the first-class game, made the 1908 side very strong in batting. Patsy Hendren and the Hon C. N. Bruce played for the first time, but only in a handful of games. The strength came from the leading occasional amateurs and from the foundation of Warner and Tarrant, whose combined average gave the side more than 100 runs an innings. Two amateurs, Moon and Page, were more than just occasionals that summer. Moon, playing 16 times and making 918, averaged 38, and Page, 687 in 15 games, averaged nearly 33. Bosanquet had 661, with two centuries, at 50.8. Sixteen centuries were scored, five each by Warner and Tarrant, who was again the leading bowler, followed by Mignon, whose 50 wickets cost 20.5 each. That was in fact his best average. Trott was well down in both lists, and there was to be no revival for him before he dropped out in 1910.

Though MacGregor had departed, Murrell kept wicket in fewer than half the games. Moon was the stumper in eight, and Page and Bird in one each. It was in the following season that Murrell began to enjoy undisputed possession of the post. As his keeping grew in stature his batting skill tended to decline.

Despite Tarrant, the bowling was not strong enough to lift the county above fourth position with six wins in 19 championship matches. They began the season with a total of 502 for nine wickets against Hampshire. Warner, 110, and Tarrant, 157, made 203 for the first wicket. That was one of four opening stands of more than 150 in which Warner took part. The others in partnership with Moon were 212 against Sussex at Lord's – a match in which Ranjitsinhji, playing in London for the first time since 1904, scored 153 not out and 78 – 161 against Nottinghamshire and 158 against Hampshire in the return match at Bournemouth. The largest total of their season was 596 against Somerset, when fast and furious scoring entertained spectators at Lord's. Moon, Bosanquet and Page made centuries, and there were three galloping stands. Bosanquet and Moon, each making

135, put on 227 in two hours, and Page, who made his 164 in 110 minutes, was the inspiration of the others, 149 with E. S. Littel-john and 92 in 40 minutes for the tenth wicket with Mignon. A third total above 500 was their 534 for eight declared against Nottinghamshire, starting with the 161 stand between Warner and Moon. James Douglas followed with 80, Tarrant with 144, and together they hit 160 in 90 minutes.

Middlesex lost one match each to Surrey and Yorkshire and drew the others. Lees and Hitch for Surrey and Hirst and Rhodes for Yorkshire were the winning bowling combinations. Kent also had a convincing win by 117 runs but with only ten minutes to spare, thanks to Frank Woolley who in 35 minutes took the last six wickets for eight. They had, too, a very tight finish at Bristol, where they got home by two runs after Gloucestershire had approached within five runs of victory with three wickets to fall. Tarrant had one of his best all-round matches, an innings of 152 and 12 wickets for 149. George Dennett, the left-arm spin-ner, was even more successful for the losers with his 13 for 120. He and his fellow left hander, Charlie Parker, did the bulk of the bowling.

The Philadelphians, who made several visits to England at this time, were on tour that summer. In their ranks was J. B. King, who was rated by his English opponents among the best fast bowlers in the world. When they met Middlesex on a pitch made treacherous by rain, the match was finished in a day. The county got home by seven wickets, and Tarrant and Trott bowled unchanged through both Philadelphian innings. Tarrant had ten wickets, Trott nine. King's bag in the two Middlesex innings was six for 30. In all 32 wickets tumbled that day for 229, and only two batsmen reached 20. Bruce made 39 and Tarrant 28. One batsman escaped the destruction. T. J. Hearne, another cousin, arrived too late to take the field at all though he was present for the final innings and would then have batted if needed. That was his only appearance for the first team, if it can be called that.

In the following season, 1909, Middlesex had another match completed in a day. At Bristol Tarrant almost defeated Glouces-tershire on his own. He took seven wickets for 18 and six for 49 to hustle Gloucestershire out for 33 and 81, and he carried his bat for 55 not out through the Middlesex innings of 145. He had, for good measure, a hat-trick in the second Gloucestershire innings.

This was another wet summer for the introduction of J. W. Hearne and Frank Mann to the county game. Of the 21 championship games ten were left drawn, and they finished in sixth position. Tarrant alone reached 1,000 runs for the county, and only Tarrant and Warner had averages in the thirties. The next figure was Robertson's 21.57. Murrell averaged just over 20, Patsy Hendren just under. Tarrant also took 108 wickets and headed both lists by a considerable margin. Although there were many helpful pitches the other bowlers did not make the most of them. J. T. Hearne's 51 wickets at 25 runs each put him second to Tarrant, but far behind the latter's 17.23 average.

That year they played only one match at Lord's in August, which was the best month for weather. So, they made a loss of £936. Such a deficit in 1971 would hardly be noticed. Indeed a county treasurer might almost consider a season in which the loss was under £1,000 as successful. At the time, however, it was regarded as disastrous. Even the one match in the comparatively good-weather month did not escape the rains. Only five hours of play were possible, and Warner batted studiously throughout for 127 not out, while Middlesex were making 307 for five wickets against the touring Australians. Warner's health was once more indifferent. Yet he made three of the county's five centuries, and Tarrant scored the others.

It was a testing season for the two newcomers. Young Jack Hearne reached double figures only once in ten innings. Then he was out of the side until the final match, when he came off for the first time by making 71 against Somerset. Mann had three games. In the first two he made 0, 5, 4 not out and 0. In the third he scored 39 and 56, also off the Somerset bowlers, but on a different occasion. Meanwhile Hendren, who had made his struggling start a year earlier, was making progress. He played regularly from the start of the season and worked his way up the batting order. He was number ten at first, then eight, seven, four and three. The outcome was a total of 698, a highest score of 75 and an average of just under 20.

D

The newcomers were needed, for Moon and George Beldam, like Bosanquet, dropped out, Wells was playing less and with less success, and Trott was close to retirement. Trott indeed played in only three matches in 1910. The refitting process, however, was made smoother by J. T. Hearne's recovery of his full powers. He took 116 wickets for the county and headed the English averages. In addition to J. W. Hearne, Hendren and Mann, the Litteljohn brothers were coming valuably into the picture, and two years later Harry Lee reached the championship side.

In both 1910 and 1911 they were third, after which they were fifth, sixth and second. And that brought them to the war. The first of those five years did not start well, for Middlesex fielded at Lord's while Kent made 500 for eight wickets. Frank Woolley, E. W. Dillon and A. P. Day made hundreds. They took a hammering from Woolley and Day during their partnership of 156 in 105 minutes. They were then bowled out, mainly by Blythe, for 105 and 197. Tarrant, Hendren and Mann were the only three who made good batting starts. Tarrant was engaged in a remarkable run of batting consistency. With the first five innings that year he actually played 34 in succession without being dismissed short of double figures. He had his usual outstanding season as an all-rounder.

Young Jack was now making rapid strides. His first century, 155 with 20 fours in three hours and three-quarters, contributed considerably to the defeat of Somerset by an innings at Lord's. His second, 108, was also part of an innings win at Eastbourne against Sussex. He took 48 wickets and had one day of remarkable bowling success at Lord's. On the first day of the match Essex were 93 for two at lunch. Afterwards their last eight fell for 17, and during this time Hearne took seven wickets in 25 balls without having a run scored off him.

Hendren, who by now had progressed to an average in the middle 20s, made his top score when Jessop, captaining Gloucestershire, sent Middlesex in first on a soft pitch. Most of the other early batsmen failed, Warner who made 40 being an exception. Hendren made 91, and J. T. Hearne and Tarrant, bowling unchanged, carried Middlesex to another innings victory. Their greatest victory was gained at Sheffield, where they rose from the depths to beat Yorkshire by 123 runs. Hirst and Booth had rattled them out for 72, and Yorkshire reached 160 for only three wickets. Middlesex were then launched on their successful, uphill fight by the two Hearnes, who caused such a collapse that Yorkshire were all out for 190. Their lead of 127 was wiped out by Warner and Tarrant in opening partnership, making 137 together. They finally set Yorkshire to make 185, and J. T. proceeded to take six wickets for 20. His match record was 12 for 65.

The other side of the picture showed Kent winning again with an innings to spare. Middlesex were unfortunate in that Kent changed their minds about their team. It had been intended that James Seymour should be the twelfth man. At the last minute he was drafted into the side to bat for four hours and three-quarters and make 193. Yorkshire beat them in a thriller at Lord's with a final innings of 331 for eight in four hours and a half, to which Hirst contributed 137. The winning runs were made off the fifth ball of what would have been the last over. The local scrap went in favour of Surrey, who won at the Oval and drew at Lord's. At the Oval Razor Smith, with a spell of six wickets for 3 in 33 balls had Middlesex out for 41 in the second innings.

The summer of 1911 was altogether more favourable for batting. In the previous year only Warner, with 44.57, and Tarrant, with 39.24, had averaged above 30 among those who played more than five innings. Now nine batmen did so, ranging from Tarrant's 50.46 to the 30.81 of James Douglas. They included the two Litteljohns, of whom A. R. bowled with remarkable accuracy and took 46 wickets in six games. Hendren scored his first century. Altogether 17 hundreds were made for Middlesex and only six against. J. W. Hearne's highest score was 234 not out against Somerset at Lord's, Tarrant and Warner each had four, and E. S. Litteljohn hit three, although he played only eight matches. The other two were made by Leonard Kidd and W. P. Harrison, one of the many occasional amateurs.

J. W. Hearne was now among the country's leading all-rounders. For the county he scored 1,447 and averaged 44.59 and also took 87 wickets, the same number as Tarrant. In the following winter he went to Australia and began his Test career.

J. T. Hearne was the leading wicket-taker – 108 at 18.09.

Warwickshire this year were the surprise champions. Middlesex in third place won 14 of their 22 championship games, and only three were left drawn. Again they were twice beaten by Kent, but they themselves beat Surrey on both occasions and outplayed them to a surprising extent. They won at the Oval in two days. The Hearnes, Tarrant and Mignon shared the wickets, and the run-getters were Hendren with 84 and Mann, who went in number eight and was 97 not out when the last wicket fell. He hit brilliantly for 150 minutes. They came out on top also against Yorkshire with an easy win and a draw very much in their favour. At Lord's E. S. Litteljohn and J. W. Hearne scored centuries and Hendren 84, when they faced a Yorkshire total of 354. They led by 71, and Tarrant and Hearne, bowling unchanged, routed Yorkshire after rain for 104. At Bradford Yorkshire were saved by the bell, for at the close they were still 141 behind and had only one wicket to fall. Tarrant played a faultless knock of 207 not out and carried his bat through an innings lasting five hours and realising 378.

The first Lancashire game at Lord's was a triumph for the Litteljohns, who were largely responsible for a Middlesex win by an innings. E. S. made 105, and A. R. took 15 wickets for 189. Lancashire won the return match, and another defeat was inflicted by Nottinghamshire in a game of tremendous scoring. It produced 1,315 runs. Joe Hardstaff senior and an amateur, G. T. Branston, scored centuries for the winners. J. W. Hearne and Warner were other century-makers, and Hendren had innings of 70 and 77.

While the batsmen were doing so well the Middlesex bowlers were not exactly out in the cold. Both Tarrant, against Somerset, and J. W. Hearne, against Essex, did the hat-trick. Murrell, too, was highly praised that summer for his wicket-keeping. In 23 matches, the extra one being against M C C, he made 54 catches and 24 stumpings.

During the following winter Warner took his second M C C team to Australia, where illness laid him low. In 1912 he was convalescing and played in only eight county games. While he was away E. L. Kidd and James Douglas led the side. As J. W.

Hearne, returning tired from the same tour, had a season of modest success, Middlesex did well in yet another damp summer to take sixth place and inflict on Yorkshire, the champions, their only defeat.

This was a low-scoring affair. It was one of Warner's few games. He was usually at his best against Yorkshire, but on this occasion he did little. The two Hearnes, Tarrant and E. S. Litteljohn were the successful players. Tarrant and J. T. Hearne had Yorkshire out for 157. Even that modest total owed most to the tail-enders, of whom Booth and Haigh put on 54 for the eighth wicket. J. W. Hearne's 60 and 38 by Murrell, going in number nine, produced a lead of 28. With the exception of Rhodes the Yorkshire batsmen again failed against Tarrant, whose six wickets for 73 gave him a match total of ten wickets. Rhodes made 84 in two hours and a half in a total of 164. Middlesex needed 139. E. S. Litteljohn scored 58, J. W. Hearne 41, and they were home by four wickets.

Only four centuries were scored for, and two against, Middlesex that summer. Both the latter were made by Essex amateurs in a high-scoring drawn match at Leyton. Percy Perrin, who has been described as the best batsman who never played for England, had 107 in the first and Charlie McGahey 117 in the second. In the same game Hendren made his highest score of the season with 97 in the second innings. All the Middlesex centuries were made at Lord's. Although he played so little, Warner scored two of them, against Lancashire and Sussex. The others were by E. S. Litteljohn against Hampshire and Tarrant against Essex. J. W. Hearne's best was his 60 against Yorkshire.

Bowling feats were more numerous than batting. In the two Surrey games little more than two days' play was possible. On both occasions wickets tumbled continuously. In the only full day at the Oval 23 fell for 283. On the other two there was enough time only for the capture of seven more wickets for 107. Razor Smith took eight wickets for Surrey, and Middlesex were put out for 194 and 129. Tarrant was top scorer with 41. The best for Surrey, who were hurried out for 67 by J. T. Hearne and Tarrant, was 18 by M. C. Bird. Hobbs was run out for 11. At Lord's 25 wickets fell in a day for 253. Surrey were all out for

52 – Tarrant five wickets for 28 and the senior Hearne five for 18. Tom Rushby then took eight for 31, and Middlesex could muster only 74. At the close of the first day Surrey were 127 for five in their second innings, and the last two were washed out.

That watery summer there were 23 completed innings under 150, ten by Middlesex and 13 by their opponents. The averages tell the story. Of those who played at all regularly Tarrant alone topped 30, and that only fractionally. The next three were Hendren averaging 27, J. W. Hearne and Haig 24 each. Haig was then played as a batsman and bowled only occasionally. The bowlers thrived. Tarrant, the largest wicket-taker, finished on 14.25, J. T. Hearne, who did the hat-trick against Warwickshire, had an average of 15.59, and J. W. Hearne of 16.76. Harry Lee, playing for the side for the first time, did nothing with the bat, but as a steady change bowler took eight wickets for 76 in four matches.

Batsmen were better suited by the conditions of 1913, though the weather upset one experiment. At that time matches started on Mondays and Thursdays. That summer two were scheduled to start on Saturdays – against Hampshire at Lord's and against Surrey at the Oval. Rain on both occasions washed out the first day's play. Other games experimentally set to start on a Friday fared better.

Young Jack Hearne was right back to form and finished far in front of the other batsmen, his county aggregate being 1,663 with an average of almost 52. Warner was next with 41, closely followed by Tarrant, and for the first time Hendren's runs for Middlesex alone exceeded 1,000. Hearne had four centuries, Warner and Tarrant three each, Hendren two, and M. H. C. Doll and Mann one each. That was Mann's first century, hit in typical manner when the side was in serious trouble against Worcestershire at Lord's. The first five wickets were down for 39 when he began his innings. While 199 were added Mann scored 135 in 165 minutes with two sixes and 18 fours. He was last out after putting on 68 for the last wicket in 40 minutes with Mignon, whose share was ten.

Once more Kent, the new champions, beat Middlesex twice. They got home by only five runs at Lord's, but at Maidstone their margin was seven wickets. That match was played on a sticky wicket, and 33 wickets fell for 285. The bowlers had a great time, J. T. Hearne and Tarrant for the losers and the left-arm spinners, Blythe and Woolley, for Kent. In the two Middlesex innings, totalling 56 and 86, Blythe took 11 wickets for 65 and Woolley seven for 62.

Immediately after that experience the county took part at Southampton in their highest-scoring match of the year. Hampshire led off with 384, of which Bowell made 130, and Middlesex replied with 548 for eight wickets declared, their highest of the year. J. W. Hearne batted four and a half hours for 189. With Hendren, whose score was 93, he put on 163 in 90 minutes. Though 1,277 runs were scored in the match, Tarrant had splendid bowling figures, five for 100 and six for 76. He almost bowled Middlesex to victory. When the eighth Hampshire wicket fell in the second innings at 156, they were still 9 runs behind. However, amateur H. C. McDonell, and Hampshire's most famous bowling partnership, Kennedy and Newman, so long defied Tarrant and company that Hampshire were able to make a token declaration and get the opposition batting again. McDonell and Newman added 45, after which Newman and Kennedy scored 91 without being parted for the last wicket.

Tarrant's best batting match was probably at Liverpool, where Lancashire gained such a decisive advantage from batting first that they won with an innings to spare. Middlesex were dismissed for 125 and 159 by the Lancastrian professionals Dean, Huddleston and Heap, who had eight wickets for 28 in the first innings. On a difficult pitch Tarrant first made 58 and then carried his bat through the second innings for 81. The next best aggregate was the 50 made in the two attempts by Saville, the hockey international. The Surrey serial favoured Middlesex. They won at Lord's, where Tarrant took 13 wickets, and at the Oval Surrey were saved by a great innings of 144 not out by Hobbs. He so dominated the proceedings after Surrey followed on 211 behind that the second-to-top score was only 29 by E. G. Goatly, who was for many years between the wars the dressing-room attendant at the Oval.

In 1914 Middlesex were runners-up to Surrey. They were

probable champions when war broke out and deprived them of important players including Warner, for their match with York-shire at Sheffield. There a weakened side were beaten by two wickets. That was their second defeat of the season, and it enabled Surrey to nose ahead. Surrey were standing first when they cancelled their final two matches on account of the war, the Oval having already been commandeered, as it was also in the Second World War. MCC ruled that Surrey were none the less the champions, and Middlesex concurred.

That 1914 side has fair claims to be considered the county's strongest. Distinguished by their several big stands Tarrant and J. W. Hearne had their greatest seasons in county cricket. They stood together at the top of the batsmen and of the bowlers. In 22 matches Hearne made 2,021 with seven centuries and an average of 74.85. Tarrant had five centuries, and his total of 1,743 gave him an average of 51.26. His bowling average of 18.4 with 131 wickets was great bowling in a generally dry season. Hearne was second at 21.42, and his wickets numbered 114. They were outstanding, but there was sound batting support for them from Robertson, Hendren, who hit three centuries, several other amateurs, and Lee, who came to his first century with 139 against Nottinghamshire. The all-round strength of the side was indicated by the list of centuries: 19 for the county and only six against. Tarrant and Hearne did not leave much for the other bowlers to do, but J. T. Hearne was still in excellent form, averaging much the same as J. W., though he was required to bowl fewer than half the number of overs that Tarrant delivered in that busy season. And several others, including now Haig, made valuable contributions.

In his book *Vintage Elevens* A. A. Thomson gave pride of place in Middlesex to the 1947 team, who won the championship under Walter Robins. He also considered Warner's championship-winning team of 1920 and the earlier champions of 1903. All three were undoubtedly strong sides. The difficulty is to estimate the precise value of the performances of the winning sides of immediate post-war years. That English cricket was weak for a few seasons after 1919 and again after 1946 was made clear by the results in Test cricket against Australia. After both wars England were trampled under foot. After the first England did not gain a single success against Australia until 1925. After the second a more or less similar period passed before the first win in Melbourne in 1951. It will be argued that Australia emerged from both wars surprisingly powerful in cricket. Yet Armstrong's sides in 1920 and 1921 were surely no stronger than Australia's under Woodfull in the thirties, when Bradman and Ponsford, Grimmett and O'Reilly were the giants. Bradman's team in the late forties could similarly be matched by the strength of Benaud's sides in the late fifties.

Warner's team of 1914 were heading for the championship until the outbreak of war destroyed their hopes. Nevertheless, being runners-up that year, when English cricket was so powerful, was probably better than being champions subsequently, when it was temporarily weak.

There were several powerful opponents in 1914, and Middlesex played them all. They did not benefit from easily-gained points against the weakest counties. Northamptonshire and Leicestershire, for instance, did not figure on their fixture list. Surrey showed their might against Middlesex. In five and a half hours on the first day at the Oval they scored 502 for six wickets against the bowling of Haig, J. T. and J. W. Hearne and Tarrant, augmented by two amateurs, H. W. Weston and Kidd. Only Hobbs among the first eight batsmen was dismissed for fewer than 35. Tom Hayward made 46, Hayes 67, Harrison 68, Ducat 102, C. T. A. Wilkinson 135 – his scoring rate was 70 an hour – Fender 51 and Hitch 35. The Surrey bowlers were Hitch, Rushby, Kirk, Fender and Hayes. A great second innings of 191 not out by J. W. Hearne not only gave Middlesex an honourable draw, but at the close they were 116 ahead with five second-innings wickets still to fall. In the return match, when Hobbs was Surrey's leading scorer, Middlesex had the better of a second draw. Yorkshire inevitably were powerfully represented throughout the period. There was always a player coming along to make good the loss when a star retired. Indeed all the then big six, Yorkshire, Surrey, Lancashire, Nottinghamshire, Kent and Middlesex, provided searching tests for any opponents.

Kent were the hoodoo side for Middlesex at that time, and

now they inflicted on them their only defeat before the weakened side fell to Yorkshire. The bowling, and more particularly the catching, let Middlesex down at Maidstone. The pitch was always difficult, but some half-dozen missed catches allowed Kent to reach 265. Kent were not so obliging, and once more Blythe and Woolley bowled them to defeat, and that by an innings. However they overcame the hoodoo in their final match that season, when Tarrant and J. T. Hearne played championship cricket for the last time. They finished in style, for Kent were bowled out for 116 and 67. Tarrant and J. T. bowled unchanged in the first innings. In the second, when Woolley hit 40 of the meagre total, they accepted help from Haig and J. W. Hearne, who had already made his mark on the game by scoring 118 not out while Middlesex were scoring 205 in their first innings. The victory margin was 298.

So Middlesex ended the period in magnificent form. Tarrant had a tremendous match at Old Trafford scoring 14 and 101 not out and taking 16 Lancashire wickets for 176. Lancashire suffered much from the pair, for it was in the game at Lord's that Tarrant and J. W. shared their record stand of 380. Hearne's best all-round match was against Essex at Lord's where he took five wickets in each innings and played innings of 88 and 37 not out.

Remarkable though their achievements were, Middlesex were far from being a two-man show. No fewer than 16 batsmen played innings of 50 or over. Of those who played only occasionally G. L. Hebden took a century off the hapless Lancashire bowlers. The highest scores of others were A. R. Litteljohn, 66 not out; Twining, 72 not out; Weston, 79 not out; the Hon R. Anson, 97; and Saville, 59. Robertson, who was able to play 11 games, made 130 against Nottinghamshire and averaged 38.66. The side had batting strength in large quantity and all the bowling that was required. Evidence that this was the best Middlesex side ever is strong.

4 Players of the Hendren Era

When county cricket was resumed in 1919 after an interval of four years, numerous familiar names were missing. Tom Hayward and Ernie Hayes were no longer in the Surrey championship side. Kent had suffered a grievous loss when Colin Blythe was killed, and their fast bowler, Fielder, was also finished with county cricket. Their bowling for some time was done very largely by the spinners, Woolley and Freeman, who not infrequently opened the bowling together. Middlesex, of course, were now without Tarrant and J. T. Hearne, and some who had been prominent before the war, though unable to play often, had fallen in action. Among them were Moon, Napier and Hunt.

Though the loss of Tarrant and Hearne could not possibly be made good quickly, the county was highly successful in the early post-war seasons, with the exception of 1919. In that year county championship matches were played over two days. The players had to toil seven hours on the first day and seven and a half on the second. Stamina was quite as important as skill. Many of the matches inevitably were left drawn, and the two-day experiment was abandoned after one season. Middlesex played only 14 championship matches, winning two and drawing nine. They also had two three-day games, against the Australian Imperial Forces and Surrey, and both those were also drawn.

J. W. Hearne and Hendren were the foundation of the post-war side. Hendren bounded to the the front. His early post-war batting was brilliantly daring and audacious, glorious stroke play based on his twinkling footwork. In 1921 he shed much of the audacity, his confidence perhaps shaken by his experiences against Gregory and Macdonald. Yet, if he no longer wielded his bat like a rapier and batted with more respect for the opposing bowlers, his scoring was soon even more prolific. Hearne was not in form with the ball in the immediate post-war season, for he was handicapped by a damaged finger. He was also troubled in these years by ill-health and in 1921 he played in only one of the Tests. Three years later, while on his third tour of Australia, ill health again handicapped him. Nevertheless, he continued to be a great force in county cricket, and some of his partnerships with Hendren rivalled those he had shared with Tarrant.

Of the other pre-war professionals Murrell and Lee remained. Murrell long maintained the standard of his wicket-keeping. Lee made rapid strides. He had been wounded and taken prisoner during the war, but he returned to cricket in 1919 a much more mature player. In the 16 matches of 1919 he and Hendren were the only two batsmen to exceed 1,000, and he continued for a time to bowl valuably. His bowling contribution to the winning of the championship in the next year was 40 wickets at 24 runs each. He was soon to have a new partner, H. L. Dales, a sound amateur opener, with whom he shared numerous good stands.

The first important newcomer, however, was Greville Stevens, who played for the Gentlemen at Lord's in 1919 while he was still a schooboy at University College School in London. In that match he batted number ten and scored 24 and 11. He also took one wicket. For Middlesex that year he played nine matches, in which he made 198 runs, his top score being 62 against Surrey, and took 24 wickets at 25.54 each. That actually put him second in the list to S. M. Haslip, who played in only five games and took 12 wickets.

Stevens was a batsman of classic style who made the most of his height in both front- and back-foot play, and who bowled leg-breaks and googlies. He was an outstanding all-rounder in the Oxford side, and between 1926 and 1930 he played ten times for England, performing a useful role in the recovery of the Ashes at the Oval in the former years. His career was comparatively short, for he was not an amateur who could devote his time to the game. Nonetheless he ranks high among the Middlesex players of the years between the wars, and his part in helping to win the championship in 1920 was considerable.

He was one of a number of leg spin bowlers who came to the

front in this time. The next was Walter Robins, who first went to Lord's as a schoolboy in 1924. He made 97 and 0 for The Rest against the Lord's Schools, then opened the innings for the Public Schools against the Army and was dismissed for 1 and 0. He did not bowl, and was still exclusively a batsman when he played in the same games a year later. And when he did bowl at that time he was a medium pacer; in that he resembled Freddie Brown. Both of them started bowling leg breaks while at Cambridge. Robins learned the tricks of the trade so quickly that in 1929 he played for England against South Africa, and he took five wickets in his first Test. He was a dashing type of cricketer, a splendid fielder, and an attacking batsman, whose running between wickets was a delight to watch.

His eagerness to take sharp runs was sometimes too much for more sedate partners. During the third Test of the 1936-7 series with Australia he joined Leyland at 195 for six wickets down. England were then 493 runs away from victory. Robins had been dismissed for a duck in the first innings. He scampered a sharp single to avoid a pair and continued to take daring runs. That was not to the liking of Leyland, who expected to make large scores and did not believe in wearing himself out between the wickets. At last, at the end of an over, Leyland walked down the pitch and told his eager partner to 'take it a bit more easily. We've got all day tomorow to make these runs.' In fact they did put on 151, Leyland contributed 111 not out, and Robins 61, and enabled England to put a better face on defeat than had seemed likely.

Robins as a batsman was handicapped by an excessively high back lift. His pick-up carried it far above his head, and from such a position strokes are apt to be hurried, particularly against fast bowling and on awkward pitches. Aubrey Faulkner, South Africa's greatest all-rounder and one of the best coaches the game has known, tried to cure the fault at his indoor school at Waltham Green in London. He tried everything, including stretching a plank of wood just above shoulder height from the netting on one side to the other. The school that day was noisy with the crash of Robins's bat meeting the plank. The lofty back lift could not be cured. In spite of it, Robins was a reasonably successful

61

batsman in all classes of the game. Without it, who knows what he might have achieved?

Leg-break bowling was an important ingredient of most attacks between the wars. The bowlers concerned were of two brands. Some of the most successful spun the ball little but, by flight and the arts of slow bowling, achieved their aim. Among them were Tich Freeman, the most prolific wicket-taker of the period, and Eric Hollies. Another, who beat his opponents by going through the spinning motions but who in fact turned the ball little, if at all, was Dick Tyldesley, the heavyweight Lancastrian. All three had excellent control of length and direction. The other type spun the ball hard but were not nearly so accurate.

The Middlesex string of leg spinners belonged to the latter group. Robins gave the ball a fierce tweak. So did Ian Peebles. He learned his trade under Faulkner, who was his uncle. Peebles was almost unplayable in the indoor school. There at lively pace, rather above slow medium, he turned both leg break and googly considerably. His pace then was similar to that of Doug Wright, who also learned leg-spin bowling from Faulkner. Wright maintained that pace when he later played for Kent and England. Peebles moderated his pace and became a slow-spinner. The reason was that he found difficulty in reproducing in the open what came easily to him under cover.

Peebles was only 19 when he went with M C C to South Africa. He played in four Tests without much bowling success, but three years later he was as dangerous as any leg spinner in the country. That was the first of Bradman's great touring years, and Peebles gave him cause for deeper thought than any other English bowler. In two Tests he had nine wickets, and that winter he, Voce and Tate were the main wicket-takers during another Test series in South Africa. Peebles seemed set for a long stay in the England side, for he was the leading wicket-taker against New Zealand in the following summer. Just about then, however, he suffered injury to a muscle in his right shoulder and could find no cure. The injury persisted and, though he was always able to bowl a googly, he lost his leg-break. Even the googly was not spun with the same force. His Test career was ended when he was 23, and he could not do all that his skill had promised for Middlesex.

However, the county was always strong in leg-spin bowlers in those years. Another was the Australian all-rounder from Oxford, Reg Bettington, and still to come were Jim Sims and Tuppy Owen-Smith. Sims began as a batsman, and for a time he went in first. It was as a leg-spinner, however, that he found fame with nearly 1,600 first-class wickets before he retired after the 1952 season. He also spun the ball heavily but was more accurate than many of his breed. Whereas the amateurs came and went, Sims was the regular. He was a great favourite with the Lord's crowd, for his bowling zest was obvious, and he was wont to play swashbuckling innings.

Owen-Smith was one of the truly great all-round games players. He took to all games naturally. He hit a century for South Africa against England at Leeds when he was 20. After that he went to Oxford and won Blues at cricket, rugger and boxing, and could have had others, if he had had the time. From Oxford he went to St Mary's Hospital in London and qualified for Middlesex while becoming a doctor. He was lost to Test cricket, but he became an international rugger player for England, and was surely one of the best full-backs in that game's history. As a cricketer he was cast in the Middlesex amateur tradition. His batting could be very brilliant, and while he was going down the pitch his speed of footwork was such that he could murder slow-spinners. That speed of foot also made him one of the outstanding fielders of the time.

In the 21 summers between the wars Middlesex had, therefore seven distinguished leg-spinners: Hearne, Stevens, Bettington, Robins, Peebles, Owen-Smith and Sims. All except Bettington were international cricketers. There lay the strength of their bowling, augmented by the contrast of speed.

The first of the fast bowlers was Fred Durston, a man cast in a massive mould. His rise was swift. In the first post-war year he took five wickets, and they cost 74 runs each. A year later he and Hearne were the two bowlers who played the main part in taking the championship to Lord's. Both took more than 100 wickets for the county, and Durston's average was down to 20 runs a wicket. Meanwhile Haig developed into a successful swing-bowler of medium-quick pace, and in the twenties Gubby Allen, probably the fastest of all Middlesex bowlers, arrived via Eton and Cambridge. Allen had one of the most perfect actions imaginable. He was not a big man, but that beautifully geared run-up and delivery enabled him to bowl in the express class. With Larwood and Voce he helped to form an exceptionally menacing, fast-bowling attack during the body-line tour of Australia in 1931-2, although Allen himself had no part in the body-line tactics, to which he was opposed. Like so many amateurs of the time his cricket was intermittent, but he played 22 Tests before the Second World War, and afterwards he was lured from retirement to lead England in the West Indies. When he first came into the first-class game, his batting was a minor consideration. By the time he became a Test cricketer, however, he was a genuine all-rounder.

Allen was a very fine cricketer, better at playing than at administration. He eventually succeeded Warner as the elder statesman at Lord's and in the Middlesex club, but he did not have comparable qualities. Allen was not such a good judge of players, and his tour of Australia as captain in 1936-7 might have had a different result with wiser team selection. Bowes, who was then at the height of his bowling powers, and Paynter, who had been a conspicuous success during the previous tour, were both left out. It was always accepted that the skipper was responsible for those northern experts not being chosen. Together they might well have tilted the scales, when England were losing the last three Tests after having won the first two.

In the thirties Middlesex had a third bowler of emphatic pace, Jim Smith, whom they obtained from Wiltshire. Smith was even larger than Durston, a giant of a man, and as genial as so many very large men are. He was a lion-hearted, fast bowler and a prodigious hitter with the bat. Big Jim relied on one great scything stroke. His left leg was moved in the direction of mid-on while he swung the bat into what used to be called the cow-shot. The ball he hammered most surely was the straight one of good length, and opposing bowlers gave him enough of those to enable him to hit with tremendous power and score on occasions at breakneck speed. Two of his most spectacular knocks were played within ten days of each other in 1938. The first was against

Sussex at Lord's on the Saturday of the Whitsun holiday, when the crowd was in the region of 30,000. Smith went to the wicket 20 minutes before the close, when the Middlesex total was already near 500. Five minutes later his score was five. In the next 15 minutes he hammered another 64, including six sixes, three of which deposited the ball in the St Johns Wood Road. His next firework display took place at Bristol. He raged to 50 in 11 minutes, and his full innings of 66, which included eight sixes, was completed in 18 minutes.

The Middlesex totals on those two occasions were 577 and 573. The first was made on the opening day of the match, but it is interesting to note that Sussex bowled 143 overs in the six hours. A comparison with any match played 30 years later would reveal how greatly the tempo of the game had changed for the worse.

The flow of amateurs continued during the years between the wars. At the start of the period, Bruce, Mann, Kidd, Twining, Crutchley, C. H. L. Skeet, Stevens, Nigel Haig, the Hon R. Anson and Dr C. H. Gunasekara, an all-rounder who was one of the best cricketers ever in Ceylon, did much to bolster the professional strength. The Hon C. N. Bruce, later Lord Aberdare, was the most naturally gifted among them and played some brilliant innings. Shortly afterwards Hugh Dales joined them and scored consistently in partnership with Lee. There followed the Robins-Peebles-Allen group, among whom were John Guise and Tom Killick, two batsmen of high quality from Cambridge. Killick played for England while still at the University. Neither played as much as the county could have wished. Guise devoted himself to the movement which was first known as the Oxford Movement and finally as Moral Rearmament. Killick went into the Church.

Again Cambridge was a fruitful source of Middlesex recruits. From that University also came H. J. Enthoven, an all-rounder who might not have been far from the Test side, if he had been able to continue regularly in the game. Later John Human shone briefly before settling in Australia. From Oxford, in addition to Owen-Smith, Middlesex for a short time had Dr Reg Bettington and then George Newman. Bettington was among the best all-rounders in the country while at Oxford. He played some cricket

E

for the county after studying to be a doctor and before returning
to his own country to play for New South Wales. Newman was
a hard-driving and successful batsman playing for the county on
occasions in the thirties.

The greatest influx of professionals came during the later years
of the period. Fred Price then proved a worthy replacement
behind the stumps for Murrell, and by 1939 professionals out-
numbered the amateurs. Sims, Smith, Denis Compton, Edrich,
Robertson, Brown and Gray were regulars that season. Hulme
and Hart played in half the matches and Thompson, Muncer and
Leslie Compton occasionally. Denis Compton and Edrich
followed Hearne and Hendren as the Middlesex twins. They did
big things before the Second World War and still bigger things
after it, both for Middlesex and England.

Edrich was one of a prolific Norfolk family of cricketers. The
Edrichs spread through the land. Bill joined Middlesex. Two
others represented Lancashire and another played for both Kent
and Glamorgan. From among the next generation John
joined Surrey and rivalled the batting feats of Bill. The latter
became qualified for championship cricket in 1937. In each of the
next three seasons he scored more than 2,000 runs and was one
of the five 'cricketers of the year' in the 1940 edition of *Wisden*.
No batsman had ever had three such opening years but, although
Edrich was only 21 in 1937, he was an experienced player. He
had played five seasons for Norfolk in minor-county cricket and
scored nearly 1,900 runs. In 1935 he had made 79 and 111
for the Minor Counties against the touring South African team,
who that year won the Test series by virtue of a great win at
Lord's. Moreover, while qualifying for Middlesex, he played
some notable innings for M C C.

Among his early feats for his new county were innings of 175
and 73 not out against Lancashire at Lord's. *Wisden* regarded
the 73 as probably the best played by anyone during the season.
After rain on the Lord's pitch the ball flew alarmingly, and the
other Middlesex batsmen were routed by Booth and Phillipson.
The total was 151. Edrich was never visibly perturbed by fast
bowling even on fiery pitches. Keith Miller said that there was
no profit in bowling bouncers at Edrich. If they were good ones,

he let them fly past and was not disturbed. If they were not good, he cracked them to the boundary.

Edrich could well have played Test cricket against New Zealand in 1937, when his cricketing twin, Compton, had his first international match. He did play against Australia the next summer, after he had completed 1,000 runs before the end of May, in company with Bradman. He had a run of low scores in the Tests but, because he was a grand fielder anywhere and also useful as an energetic quick bowler, he played throughout the series and also toured South Africa the following winter. There his run of low scores continued until the last innings of the final Test, when he hit 219. Such is the way of selectors, who had stuck by him while he was failing, that, once he had proved their point and demonstrated his Test quality, he was dropped. He was not chosen for any of the 1939 Tests against the West Indies, although he was again in great batting form.

Off the field Edrich did not always take his training as seriously as he might have done. On it, however, he was a tremendous trier, who would never yield. When his chance again came to prove himself in Test cricket, he did so in the hardest possible school, against the Australian bowling of Lindwall, Miller and company. For long it seemed that the selectors would ignore his claims in 1946. It was not until the last Test against India that he was recalled, and he was a late selection for the Australian tour, on which he, almost alone, held the batting together in the early Tests while Hutton and Compton were out of touch.

The one obvious cricketing flaw in the make-up of the twins was their running between wickets. There may have been more unreliable pairs of runners, but there cannot have been many. Their misunderstanding was sometimes complete. Compton defended himself by saying that he ran himself out as often as he did his partner – which was quite true.

Compton, being qualified by birth, preceded Edrich into the county side. He could be said to have started at the bottom and worked his way up, which he did at a remarkably rapid rate. After playing three times for the second team in 1935 without distinction, he was brought into the championship side soon after his 18th birthday in the following season. The occasion was the Whitsun match with Sussex, his batting place number 11. There he batted well and importantly, for his 14 contributed to a last-wicket stand of 36 with Allen, which gave Middlesex first-innings points in a drawn match of low scoring.

The manner of his innings created an impression out of all proportion to its size, and he was promptly pushed up the order. He was number eight in the next match against Nottinghamshire, then seven for his third, in which he scored 87 and rescued the side in the second innings, when Northamptonshire had taken the first five wickets for 21. Soon he was number three and scoring 77 against Hampshire, and he was already a fixture among the first five in the order. Although he did not start until the end of May and left before the season's end to play football with the Arsenal, he completed 1,000 in his first year. He was second to Hendren among the regulars in the averages with 35.32. He had also made his first century in cavalier fashion with 100 in 105 minutes in the return match with Northamptonshire.

After that first season Plum Warner said he was 'the best young batsman who has come out since Hammond was a boy'. The rapidity of his maturity was exceptional. Everything he did was natural, and his instinct was his surest guide. Len Hutton, the other very great batsman of his generation, often used to reach the same conclusion as Compton. The difference was that Hutton used his astute cricket brain to arrive at it, whereas Compton got there intuitively without thought.

Already in his teens Compton looked the complete batsman and a superb fielder. He had all the strokes. He had the footwork and the confidence to use it far from the crease against slow bowlers, and sometimes against those who were not so slow. The only criticism of his batting in 1936 made by *Wisden* concerned his footwork when hooking. 'This did not affect the stroke itself,' the *Almanack* recorded, 'but it often threatened the loss of his wicket, as it did at Hove when he trod on his stumps.' Again the adjustment came instinctively, and he was soon one of the game's best and most daring hookers. Daring was an integral part of his batsmanship, and he was well equipped to exploit it. If his judgement ever failed him, he was a master at improvising and contriving an escape, helped by the sure speed of his footwork.

Compton has his own strokes. It seems inevitable that, when a great player has an unusual stroke peculiar to him, that is what most players seek to imitate, ignoring all in his play which could more safely and profitably be borrowed. It was so with the Compton sweep to long leg. Compton's bat played it with much profit. Many lesser mortals were not as successful. He had indeed strokes all round the wicket, and his off-driving covered a wide arc. Balls pitching in the same place might travel anywhere between the bowler and third man, depending on how he used his wrists. The positioning of the left foot gave him wide scope in this stroke, for he did not observe the book advice to move it to the pitch of the ball. He planted it well inside the line of the ball, as most of the best Australian batsmen do. English batsmen tend to be more orthodox, Colin Cowdrey for instance. His left foot is so correctly placed, according to the book of instruction, that his bat can drive it only in one direction. Placing the off-side field for a Cowdrey is therefore easier than for a Compton.

In his second season, aged 19, Compton set out on his Test career. He and Washbrook played their first matches for England against New Zealand at the Oval. Washbrook was not immediately successful. Compton was. But for being run out, he might well have launched himself into the international field with a century. Run out? Yes, but it was not his fault on this occasion. He was batting with Hardstaff, together adding 125 after the first three wickets had gone for 36, when his partner drove the ball straight down the pitch. Vivian, the bowler, half-stopped it and deflected it in to the wicket. Compton was backing up and could not regain his crease in time. However, he had made 65 inside two hours, and selection for the next summer's Tests against Australia was virtually assured. The first of his 17 Test hundreds came in his first match against Australia; and that season before he came of age, he was one of *Wisden*'s five cricketers of the year.

When he first played for Middlesex Compton also filled in as an orthodox left-arm spinner. After the war he developed the googly and the left-hander's off-break, the 'chinaman' as it was called for no clear reason. If length and direction were variable, he got a tremendous amount of work on the ball, and the wickets he took did nearly as much to win the county their post-war championship as the many, many runs he made.

The figures of the Middlesex twins are impressive indeed. In 78 Tests Compton made 5,807 runs and averaged just over 50. In all first-class cricket his total was 38,942, and only three Englishmen – Hammond, Sutcliffe and Hutton, who figure among those with 30,000 runs – have exceeded his average of 51.85. His centuries numbered 123. For good measure he took 620 wickets. Edrich played in 39 Tests, hit six centuries and had a total of 2,440 with an average of 40. His centuries in all first-class cricket totalled 86, and his 36,965 runs gave him an average of 42.39. He also took 479 wickets and made many brilliant slip-catches. Moreover he scored a century in his final first-class innings, when turning out for M C C against Cambridge in 1958. After that he enjoyed a new lease of cricketing life and began yet another career with his native Norfolk. Years afterwards he came back to Lord's with Norfolk for a Gillette Cup match and was his side's most successful batsman.

Compton was an outside-left for Arsenal. At football also his instinct served him well. He was not really a top-liner. He missed the class of his brother Leslie, but he had the knack, born of instinct, of being in the right position at the right time to snatch the vital goal. Denis played for England in a war-time international. Leslie, full-back and centre-half, was a full international. So was a third Arsenal-Middlesex player, Joe Hulme. He was a flier on the right wing, a thrilling sight when in full flight and hardly less so when racing round the boundary on the cricket field. In the thirties he did yeoman service with the bat and as a sure, speedy fielder. One of his best seasons was Denis Compton's first, when he had four centuries, scored 1,127 and averaged 35.21.

George Hart was another professional of somewhat similiar cricketing qualities. He never quite established himself in the side, though he played 23 matches in 1936 and topped 900 runs. There were also other professionals who played on occasions in addition to those mentioned, such as Powell, Beton, North, Fowler, Watkins and Nevell. One who did establish himself was Laurie Gray, a persistent bowler of medium-quick pace, who was a good second string to Jim Smith in the late thirties and who after the war plugged away with Edrich. Fred Price, of course, had long since succeeded Murrell as the wicket-keeper, and he maintained his high standard until the late forties, in addition to batting valuably.

There were also many itinerant amateurs, for the county continued to encourage them throughout the period. At times it seemed that the effectiveness of the side was adversely affected by the inclusion of a young amateur from the universities, late in the season, at the expense of a professional who had been pulling his weight. Cricketers such as Len Muncer could have otherwise played more often just before the Second World War. The fine work Muncer afterwards did for Glamorganshire as an all-rounder might then have been done for Middlesex instead.

Muncer was an orthodox spin-bowler of off-breaks. Between the wars Middlesex had little bowling of that type. Their slow bowling was done almost exclusively by the leg-spinners. The change followed the war. Jack Young, who played occasionally before it, became the main bowler, and he was an orthodox-left-arm spinner.

Those then were the players who guided Middlesex between the wars. History has a habit of repeating itself. It certainly has in the case of Middlesex history. Before the First World War they were building to a climax. After it they proceeded to win the championship twice. At the end of that 20-year period they were again knocking hard at the door then held firmly shut by the great Yorkshire side. After the interval caused by the war the championship was again speedily taken twice to Lord's. On the former occasion Hearne and Hendren had blossomed and were ready to carry the county in the post-war years. In 1939 Compton and Edrich were similarly poised. The championship successors were followed both times by a period of comparatively modest achievement. We may have reason for national apprehension, if we see signs of another pair of Middlesex twins appearing on the cricket scene.

5 Warner's Final Triumph, 1920

If Middlesex could do no better than finish 13th in 1919, it was not a season from which to draw firm conclusions. The batting was strong. The bowling, with Hearne handicapped by a finger injury, was weak. Hearne was, nevertheless, the leading wicket-taker with 43, but they were unusually expensive, costing 34 runs each. Gunasekara took 36 and Haig 30. The most encouraging bowling event was the success of Greville Stevens with his 24 wickets at reasonable cost. Lee helped with the wicket-taking, and Hendren was also pressed into service. His 15 at 37.20 placed him close to Hearne in the averages. The next season, when the attack had found itself, Patsy bowled in only one match and took one wicket.

Hendren and Hearne were also together in the batting list, but in reversed order. Hendren took the first opportunity to advertise his rise to the front rank. There he was to stay year after year, and the time came when he was not far off representing half the county's batting strength. For Middlesex that summer he made 1,258, and in all first-class cricket he was second to George Gunn with a total of 1,655 and an average of 61.29. Hearne occupied seventh position with 1,380 at nearly 50 an innings. Harry Lee followed them, averaging just over 40 and scoring 1,000 in the county's 16 games. That was to be the pattern for some seasons with Hendren and Hearne as the stars and Lee as their main supporter.

Warner captained the side in 11 matches, but his only considerable score was 101 retired against the formidable Australian Imperial Forces team. Pre-war players predominated, and they included Bosanquet and Robertson. Each played six times with success. Bosanquet hit his top score of 82 at Old Trafford against Lancashire, who had in Cecil Parkin the most dangerous bowler in the first-class game, and in the next match he made 51 against Yorkshire. Murrell had a good season with the bat and behind the stumps, but Mann had only a modest one giving him an average of 21.

Bruce had not played for the county since 1908. His return for the match against Lancashire at Lord's was wonderfully successful. In 145 minutes he hit 149 out of 217 without giving the semblance of a chance. There were 25 fours in an innings of rare brilliance, and in the second innings, when Middlesex were chasing victory which they could not finally achieve, he made 51 in 35 minutes.

The highest total was 608 for seven wickets declared against Hampshire, for whom Kennedy took all seven. In the absence of Jack Newman, who had not yet returned from his war service, Kennedy bowled 55 overs for 202 runs, many of them made by the twins. Hearne was 218 not out, and Hendren scored 201 in 175 minutes while they were putting on 325. Hendren hit four sixes and 21 fours. That was Hendren playing up to the brilliantly dashing standard he was to maintain in the first two post-war years. That match also contained one of the comparatively few fine bowling performances. In his first match for Middlesex Stevens took seven wickets for 104 and three for 32, and Middlesex were home by an innings and 74 runs in a game which produced 1,142 runs in under 14 hours of actual playing time.

Runs flowed also during the two days at Leyton, where Essex helped towards an aggregate of 1,097. Hendren made one of his centuries, Kidd scored 92, and Murrell 96 not out, going in number ten and putting on 152 in 75 minutes with E. Martin, one of the many occasional amateurs.

Surrey were met three times that season. In yet another game of hectic scoring Surrey won on the stroke of time by an innings at the Oval. There Andy Sandham, batting number four, made 175 not out in a total of 582 for nine wickets declared. Surrey's number 11 was W. J. Abel, nursing a strained side, in spite of which he made 73 not out and helped Sandham in an unfinished stand of 133. At Lord's the championship match was drawn, as was their three-day friendly played for charity at the Oval. Lee made a hundred in each innings, and the first four Middlesex batsmen launched the game with a string of big scores and partnerships; Robertson 52, Lee 163, Hearne 113 and Kidd 100. The last-named played only twice and made runs both times.

The championship that year turned on the Middlesex matches against the two contenders, Yorkshire and Kent. Yorkshire, their new opening pair of Holmes and Sutcliffe scoring freely and Rhodes taking wickets, won at Leeds and drew at Lord's. Hendren, unusually, was out of touch in both games, but he scored 45, 37, 37 and 40 against Kent. The first two innings did not stop Woolley, Freeman and Fairservice from bowling out Middlesex for 122 and 177 and winning by an innings at Maidstone. The return was the last match of the season, in which victory would give Kent the title. In spite of rain, which restricted play to 90 minutes on the first day, the same three bowlers almost got them home. They themselves made 196, dismissed Middlesex for 87, only Hendren and Hearne reaching double figures, and made them follow on. Despite Hendren's 40, Middlesex were still 23 behind and eight wickets down with 15 minutes remaining. At that point Saville and Mann, using attack as the best means of defence on the difficult pitch, hit 35. Middlesex finished with 121, 12 ahead, and the championship went to Yorkshire.

The other three-day game was against the Australian Services. Their touring group included six who played Test cricket against England during the next two years: Kelleway, Collins, Gregory, Pellew, Oldfield and Taylor. Middlesex played them to a level draw, leading in fact by 38, thanks to Warner and Hendren, after Collins had scored a century for the Australians. Warner made his hundred in spite of being twice seized by cramp, and finally had to be carried into the pavilion. Hendren, his partner in a fourth wicket stand of 167, made 135.

Cramp was also to be Warner's enemy during the great title-winning year of 1920. In the first championship game against Warwickshire at Lord's he went in first with Lee. They had put on 165, when Warner, then 76, had to retire yet again. However, he played right through the season, totalling 20 championship games and two others. His captaincy naturally was his greatest contribution, but his batting in his final season was far from being unimportant. He made 766, more than anyone apart from the three main batsmen, and his average was close to 30.

Their humble position in 1919 gave no hint that they were so soon to become contenders for the championship. The match-winners from first to last were Hendren, Hearne, Lee and Durston. Magnificently though they played, however, they could not have taken Middlesex to the top without being soundly supported. They had that support from the other four regulars: Warner, Murrell, Mann and Haig, and from whichever of their gifted amateurs were available. The most important of the last was Stevens. He played in 12 matches, took fourth place to the three leading batsmen and was third among the bowlers after Hearne and Durston. In championship matches his 44 wickets cost under 19 runs each. His two against a very powerful Rest of England side cost 153.

Though Hendren was even more brilliant and successful than in the previous summer, the two players who made the vast difference between the records of the two years were Hearne and Durston. Hearne fully regained his bowling, and Durston became a fast bowler of fire and stamina. The latter attribute was very important, for at the end of July there was no suggestion that they could win the title. They did so by winning their last nine matches. They could not afford to drop a single point, and the climax was reached on the last day of August, when they beat Surrey against all the odds.

The championship was decided on the percentage system: a win earned five points, and the lead in a drawn match three; games in which no first-innings result was obtained were ignored. At the end of July Middlesex were lying sixth, behind Surrey, Kent, Yorkshire, Lancashire and Nottinghamshire. The big six in fact were in force in the leading positions. Surrey's percentage was 78.65, that of Middlesex merely 58.18. From that point they moved steadily through the field. On 10 August, after three wins, they were still not above fifth, but their percentage was only ten behind that of Kent, the new leaders. Another ten days on and they were first, just ahead of Yorkshire; but Lancashire were also winning matches, and until the end of the campaign it was a tight fight with them. Middlesex were finally home with 77.00 to

Lancashire's 74.61. Of their 20 championship matches they won 15, lost two and drew three.

Even though the skipper had to retire suffering from cramp, the first match at Lord's was highly encouraging. All the main batsmen played big innings: Lee, 102; Hearne, 96 and Hendren, 158, a superb innings containing three sixes and 12 fours and lasting no more than 115 minutes. He hit two successive balls from Willie Quaife for six, the first landing the ball on the roof of the pavilion. Gunasekera took five first-innings wickets, L. V. Prentice, an amateur who played only three matches, had six in the second, and Warwickshire were beaten by an innings.

So were Sussex in the next match, which was made remarkable by the first four batsmen scoring centuries. Only three years later Middlesex were to repeat what was until then an unique performance in English cricket. The four against Sussex did not include Hendren. His position that day was number five, his contribution to a total of 543 for four wickets merely 17. Before him Warner had made 139, his last century, Lee 119, Hearne 116 not out and Haig 131 with 20 fours in 110 minutes of swashbuckling. Maurice Tate was in the Sussex attack that day, as was Arthur Gilligan, but Tate had not then started his fast-medium bowling which brought him fame. He then bowled off breaks, but was played more for his batting than his bowling.

Not content with his century, Lee went on to make sure of victory by taking five wickets for 21 and six for 47. Lee was indeed an important bowler throughout, for he took 40 wickets in the championship. So, two matches had been won by an innings, but after a draw with Lancashire the first defeat followed at the hands of Nottinghamshire. Middlesex had the worst of the pitch in a low-scoring match, and the leg-spin bowling of Richmond gave Notts a margin of 151 runs. Richmond had 11 wickets for 85, and Middlesex were put out for 98 and 108. Yet on the difficult pitch Hearne played a magnificent second innings. Going in number three all his artistry was required to resist Richmond. He made 58 not out, and Hendren's 11 was the next-highest score.

Four of the next five matches were won. Hampshire fell twice, Durston among the wickets on both occasions and Hendren making 183 not out in the first and Lee 221 not out in the second. Somerset fell, and just before them Lancashire did the same by an innings and 37 runs. Hendren had another innings of 183 not out, made in little more than three hours, and Durston and Hearne bowled the Lancastrians out twice.

Middlesex were going wonderfully well, but a serious set-back came from an unexpected quarter. They met Essex in successive matches and took only three points from the two. They had first-innings points from the game at Lord's. This was a batsman's match, 1,290 runs for 31 wickets. Hendren, 124, Hearne, 86, and Stevens 92, coming in for his first match that year, were the main Middlesex scorers. For Essex A. C. Russell made 197 and Laurie Eastman, a cheerfully adventurous cricketer, cracked 91 from his humble position at number ten.

The second match at Leyton was dominated by the bowlers, and Essex finally won by four runs, with eight minutes remaining. It was a curious game, in which Middlesex contributed to their own downfall. Murrell must have had an off-match, for in the Essex totals of 133 and 196, with Hearne taking three wickets for 33 and eight for 49, the extras numbered 25 and 32. Another oddity was the retirement of Warner during the first Middlesex innings. He had contracted to return to Lord's to help the selection of the team to tour Australia. Accordingly, when he was 22 and batting well in partnership with Lee, he retired. Afterwards only Stevens provided much support for Lee, who carried his bat throughout an innings of 212 for 80. Despite their failings Middlesex seemed set for another win, when they had to make only 118 in the final innings. The swing bowling of Johnny Douglas, however, was too much for all except Warner and Murrell. Eight were out for 67 when Murrell joined Warner and helped to add 33. While Durston defended, 11 more were scored. Then Warner was bowled by Douglas, and Middlesex were shocked losers. Douglas had kept up his pace for 24.2 overs and taken seven wickets for 47.

They were now at the end of July, far behind the leaders, as they set off on their remarkable finish. Stevens took 13 wickets for 60 to bring about the defeat of Sussex by an innings, and Hearne's second-innings eight for 26 gave them a thrilling victory by 5 runs against Kent at Canterbury. Surrey by an innings and Nottinghamshire by nine wickets were more easily overcome. Then came another spine-chiller at Bradford, which swung back and forth from start to finish. The start was on a sticky wicket, not at all unusual at Bradford, and Rhodes and Rockley Wilson had Middlesex out for 105. Then Yorkshire were in trouble against Hearne and Stevens. Middlesex looked like leading until the Yorkshire captain, D. C. F. Burton, was joined by Arthur Dolphin at 69 for seven. Burton made 36, Dolphin 52, and they gave their side what looked like being a decisive lead of 64. Though Lee, 48, and Hendren, 56, played well, Middlesex would have been out of the running, if Haig, the number seven, had not hit bravely and well for 86. In the final innings 198 were needed. One after another the Yorkshiremen got to double figures and were then winkled out by Durston, Hearne, Stevens or Haig. Nine wickets were down for 140, and only Wilson and Waddington remained. Neither had pretensions as batsmen, but on and on they went, and Middlesex were desperate when at last Stevens bowled Waddington. They had put on 53 and the winning margin was only 4 runs.

Bowlers had a great time, particularly Rhodes. He had figures of seven for 53 and three for 98, and took his total of wickets in first-class cricket to 3,000, the first bowler to do so. Wilson was the other destroyer, three wickets for 30 and six for 62. Hearne's six for 52 was the best bowling for the winners.

Somerset and Warwickshire were afterwards disposed of comfortably, and Kent were again overcome. This time the margin was greater, 153 runs with more than an hour to spare. Hendren's contribution was 170 followed by 84, and five bowlers shared the wickets. And that brought them to the final thrilling episode at Lord's involving Surrey.

By any yardstick that was a great cricket match. It catered for those who desired drama. It served also the sentimentalists, for this was Warner's last championship match, and he made a great exit. Here was another game similar in one respect to that against Yorkshire, but very different in others. It swung from side to side to test the nerve of all in the large crowds, who so packed Lord's that on each of the first two days the gates had to be closed. Even on the last day, when the figure has always dropped greatly whatever the state of a match might be, there were some 15,000 spectators.

It was first strike to Surrey. Rushby, Hitch and Fender had the first three Middlesex wickets down for 35, and, though Hendren made 41, half the side were out for 109. Warner was still there, and he battled on until he had made 79. Stevens, who scored 53, added 90 for the seventh wicket with him, but 253 for eight at the close did not offer much prospect of a win in the remaining two days. The next morning they were out for 268. Surrey made much better progress, thanks to Sandham, who went in first and batted throughout. In just under four hours and a half he made 167, and Surrey were able to declare at 341 for nine wickets. Ducat had made 49 and shared a stand of 99. Fender hit five fours in the course of a lively 30.

When Middlesex batted again, 73 down, six hours 40 minutes still remained to be played. A draw, which would send the championship to Old Trafford, seemed almost inevitable, for in their final match Lancashire were easily beating Worcestershire. Skeet, the Oxford batsman, was Lee's partner. He had done little for the county so far. Now he more than earned his keep, for the opening partners so tore into the Surrey bowling that well inside three hours 208 were scored. Lee went at that total for 108, and Skeet soon afterwards for 106. From that point Middlesex chased runs recklessly. Wickets fell but runs came, until finally Warner joined Stevens for his last innings at Lord's and they banged 25 in eight minutes. Warner, who had been emotionally received by the crowd, was 14 not out, when he then declared. The total was 316 for seven wickets, and Surrey had rather less than three hours in which to make 244. Warner had dangled a tempting carrot. Surrey went for it.

Haig had Hobbs caught in the slips at 22, the ball bouncing out of Hendren's hands and being retrieved by Lee, and at 62 Murrell stumped Miles Howell off Stevens. When Sandham and Shepherd had the score past 100 in 75 minutes, the outlook for Middlesex was black. Then at 120 Hendren took a great catch high overhead in the deep to dismiss Shepherd, and suddenly the game took its final swing. Durston's pace bowled Fender, and leg spin raged through the remaining Surrey defences. Sandham, caught and bowled by Hearne for 68, was fifth out, and Surrey's cause was hopeless. When Stevens bowled Strudwick, 40 minutes of play still remained unused, and Middlesex were victors by 55 runs. Stevens had taken five wickets for 61 and Hearne three for 37. And the crowd swirled on to the field to carry Warner shoulder-high to the pavilion.

What a season's cricket that had been, and watched by such crowds that Middlesex made a profit of £3,270. The admission charge at that time was a shilling. Others, too, did well from their match with the new champions. At the Oval nearly 24,000 people paid at the turnstiles on the first day. On the same ground nearly £1,000 was made for charity in the Champion County *v* The Rest match.

In this Middlesex held to a draw a powerful side composed of ten men – due to go on Test tour to Australia – plus Holmes. Their bowlers were mauled, for Jack Hobbs ruled supreme for 200 minutes while making 215. Russell, Ernest Tyldesley, Holmes, Woolley and Douglas also scored strongly, and The Rest declared at 603 for five wickets. The Middlesex batsmen, however, acquitted themselves well. They batted first, and scores of 60-odd by Hendren, Stevens and H. K. Longman carried them to 318, to which they finally added 192 for four, Hendren matching his first innings score, while Warner ended his career undefeated with 19.

The four leading players had great figures to reward their efforts. In all first-class games Hendren headed the national averages with 2,520 at 61.46, and Hearne was fourth with 2,148 at 55.07. Lee topped 1,500 and averaged 43.37. Hearne was highly placed among the bowlers, his total bag being 142 at 17.83, and Durston took 113. Lee's complete wicket total was 52, and Stevens, who had a highly successful season for Oxford before joining the county side, narrowly missed the double. He had 1,357 runs and 93 wickets.

6 The Hendren Era, 1921-39

Frank Mann, like his son George 27 years later, took over a flourishing concern. The championship was again won in 1921, and his reign as captain was generally smooth. Nigel Haig later had the rough time, falling between two professional generations and not regularly enjoying the amateur strength to cover the gap.

The 1921 success was achieved in spite of Hearne's renewed poor health, which reduced his bowling effectiveness but not his scoring, and although Stevens played little and with less success. The batting was again tremendously powerful. Their highest total was 612 for eight against Nottinghamshire, when Lee made 243 not out, and they had numerous other large totals. Hendren, Hearne and Lee led the scoring once more, and Twining and Bruce with his superb off-side stroke play averaged above 35. Mann hit two centuries, Crutchley and Haig one each, and Dales made his way into the side by averaging over 25.

The bowling loss of Hearne, whose tally of championship wickets was more than halved, was made good by the advance of Haig and yet another upward move by Lee, who in all matches that summer took 72 wickets at 19.66. Haig took 111, 96 of them for the county. He had started in the side, played mainly for his batting, as a tearaway bowler. Now he had harnessed the outswinger at medium-fast pace. He and Durston, who stepped up his total to 136 in all first-class cricket, formed an excellent opening attack.

The path to the championship was somewhat different, for the first eight matches were won, and they always threatened to finish first. Their chief rivals were Surrey, and each team won one of the matches in which they clashed. In this season Jack Hobbs played hardly at all. Illness kept him out in the first half. When he returned and was promptly pressed into Test service at

F

Leeds, he was stricken by appendicitis before batting and was out for the season. Without the greatest batsman of the day Surrey did well to be runners-up.

In the match at the Oval Middlesex went down by 19 runs after a great uphill fight. At one time they looked like being swamped. Hitch and Rushby had them out for 162 and gave Surrey a lead of 135, which they increased by 234 for eight. Despite Lee's 82 Middlesex slumped to 159 for six wickets. Then Stevens, who made 78, and L. L. Burtt, 50, put on 132 and the final total was 350. *Wisden* recorded that 'Burtt gave no suggestion of class in his play, but he showed great coolness.' He contributed nothing else of note to his county's history.

As in 1920 the championship was decided by the last match of the season. The difference was that Surrey had to win to take top place. Middlesex had only to avoid defeat, and for two days even that modest ambition did not look like being realized. Again they failed in the first innings, and Surrey, for whom Tom Shepherd made 128, led by 136. But they were now bowled out for 184, largely by Haig who took five wickets for 62, and Middlesex scored 322 with surprising ease. They lost only four wickets in the process. Twining and Hearne hit centuries, and their partnership of 277 was decisive. So, in the end Middlesex, who were expert that summer at turning first innings defeats into victories, finished well ahead in the championship table.

Hendren played with much less dash after his unhappy Test experiences, which in fact were similar to those of his county when they met the Australians. They were beaten in two days, feeling the fast-bowling sting of Macdonald and Gregory and being skittled for 111 and 90. In championship matches Hendren's more circumspect batting methods gave him an average of 57.6, which was 5 ahead of Hearne. In all matches, however, Hearne was 7 in front. Though Hendren exceeded 2,000 again, his overall average was down to just below 42.

A slip in the next season to seventh position was not readily explained, though that was actually better than it seems, for they were still not playing the weakest counties: Northamptonshire, Derbyshire, Worcestershire and Glamorgan, who had only recently joined the competition. Hendren increased his average to 75.5. Hearne was in better health and, back to wicket-taking, narrowly missed the double. Stevens played more often and rather more usefully. Dales made a further batting advance, and Mann played his best cricket when it was most needed. With Durston and Haig maintaining their bowling form, there was really not much difference between the number one side of 1921 and the number seven side of 1922, and they played much fine cricket. Their finest win was by eight wickets against Sussex at Lord's. The game was played on a fiery pitch and few gave them a chance of making the necessary 230 in the last innings. Hearne and Hendren upset calculations by scoring 190 together.

That year the last link with the Walkers of Southgate, who had played such a prominent part in the foundation of the club was broken by the death of R. D. Walker. For 58 years one or other of the seven brothers had held office in the club. The last of the Walkers was succeeded as president by A. J. Webbe.

Middlesex had much the same ingredients the following year when they descended one more place. Hearne did do the double that summer, although a hand injury put him out of the last seven matches. The main loss was Haig, who was ill and bowled only 15 overs late in the season. Stevens had enjoyed a splendid all-round season for Oxford, and Allen had similarly thrived at Cambridge. For the county, however, they were very disappointing. Stevens's 33 wickets cost almost 40 runs each.

Hendren had a great summer. In only 22 championship games he ran up a total of 2,263, average 87, and he headed the national averages by a large margin. He passed 3,000 for the first time and hit 13 centuries. In five days during August he had a prolific scoring run with 86 not out and 142 not out against Surrey, and 33 and 146 against Nottinghamshire. Hearne played one of the finest innings of his career against Yorkshire. Batting conditions were by no means ideal, and most of the other batsmen were well-nigh helpless against Waddington, Robinson, Macaulay, Roy Kilner and Rhodes. Only two of them, Hendren and Murrell, reached double figures while Hearne was majestically striding to an unbeaten 175 in a total of 289.

Defeats in both matches by both Yorkshire and Lancashire accounted largely for their comparatively modest position in the table. They did, however, gain a great victory at **Canterbury**, after Woolley had hit 270 and carried Kent to 445. Middlesex replied with 457 and then Kent were unaccountably dismissed on a good pitch for 159. Stevens had his best bowling match, five wickets for 41, but the direst damage was done to Kent by Guise. As a bowler he was not seriously regarded. He was brought on as fourth change at 96, for no obvious reason, and his innocuous-looking slow stuff disposed of Jack Bryan, Seymour, Woolley and Ashdown for 9 runs in 25 balls. Hendren and Mann duly saw Middlesex home by seven wickets. That season also Middlesex for the second time had four centuries hit for them in an innings. Dales, Lee, Hearne and Hendren were the batsmen against Hampshire, and the last two scored 375 together.

A year later, with Haig fit again and Stevens playing more worthily, Middlesex were back in the championship race. They finished second to Yorkshire, and until they were surprisingly defeated by Gloucestershire at Bristol they were chasing hard. That was a curious match, which started with Haig and Durston dismissing Gloucestershire for 31, after which they were in turn put out for 74. Starting in that innings the Gloucestershire performance rested on two men. Charlie Parker's left-arm spin accounted for seven Middlesex batsmen for 30. Wally Hammond, then just 21, proceeded to give what was rated by *Wisden* as ' the batting display of the year '. Inside four hours he hammered 174 runs from the Middlesex bowlers without being dismissed, and Gloucestershire were able to declare at 294 for four wickets – after which it was Parker's turn again. He took another seven, and Middlesex were out for 190.

Hendren that summer made his successful return to the Test side. He and Hearne missed several county matches, and Hendren had his least successful championship season of the decade. His aggregate was 1,095 and his average was down to 47.60, though he was so successful in other first-class cricket that he was third in the English averages to Sandham and Hobbs with 56.75. In the Test matches his scores were 74, 50 not out, 132 and 142.

The Yorkshire match at Lord's was played while a Test Trial was in progress. Hearne and Hendren on one side, Holmes, Sutcliffe, Kilner and Macaulay on the other, were missing. Mann and Stevens, partners while 151 were hit in 95 minutes, played leading roles in an innings win. Stevens scored 114. In the course of his 79 Mann hit four sixes off Rhodes, one of which landed the ball on the pavilion roof. Yet this was probably not his most spectacular hit. That was surely a straight drive he made while batting at the pavilion end at Lord's on a later occasion. The stroke might have been made by a golfer's brassie – number two wood to moderns – for the ball did not carry the sight-screen by much and yet did not pitch until it had carried half-way across the nursery ground.

A spectacular win that summer was gained at Trent Bridge after Nottinghamshire had made them follow on 209 behind. Guise then scored 100 in a total of 358, and Allen, who, like Stevens, had a much better county season, bowled Notts out for 122 by taking six wickets for 31. Dales, who, as in the previous season, exceeded 1,000 in all first-class matches, Bruce and Kidd were other amateurs who helped to minimize the handicap imposed by the absence of Hendren and Hearne.

Middlesex were sixth in each of the next two seasons. Hearne made a full contribution in the first of them, and he added the elegance of an innings of 117 to his Benefit match against Sussex, which realized £1,730. Crowds were consistently large, and in 1926 the profit on their match with the Australians was £2,640.

In that season ill-health kept Hearne out of ten games and brought his Test career to an end. Nothing, however, could stop Hendren. He had his ups and downs in Test cricket, but he was always the dominant batsman in the county side. Counting only those who played at least ten innings, Hendren was actually top of the county's championship averages for 16 years in succession. In one year Allen, playing only nine innings, exceeded his average, and finally that player, batting 14 times, edged him into second place in 1936. To do so he needed the help of five not-out innings, whereas Hendren was not out only once in 42 innings.

Scoring throughout the country had been heavy since the war, except when rain favoured the bowlers. It was becoming heavier and reached new heights in the late twenties and thirties, when it was further stimulated by Bradman. Hendren naturally played a large part in the run-getting. In 1925 he had a particularly brilliant run. In a fortnight his scores were 234 and 37 against Worcestershire, 142 against Lancashire, 240 against Kent and 10 and 206 not out against Nottinghamshire.

The last of those innings played a part in the county's most remarkable win of the summer. Nottinghamshire set them to make 502, and they got them for the loss of six wickets. Bruce made 103 and put on 154 with Hendren in 95 minutes. Finally Mann scored 101 not out while he and Hendren were hitting off the last 271 in 195 minutes. Two bad failures were against Yorkshire, who on each occasion scored more than 500 for six wickets. At Lord's Percy Holmes batted nearly seven hours for 315 not out. For a year that stood as the highest score ever made at Lord's. Then Hobbs made 316 not out.

Holmes did not open the Yorkshire innings in the return match with Middlesex at Leeds. He was delayed on the railway and arrived late. Leyland took his place and with Sutcliffe began the innings with a stand of 218. Leyland made 110 and Sutcliffe 235, for which he batted six hours and a half. That was the occasion when a northern writer, so long accustomed to seeing Holmes and Sutcliffe together, did not notice the change. Everything Leyland achieved he credited to Holmes, until he finally discovered his error at lunch. His get-out afterwards was dignified and unrepentant. 'During the lunch interval,' he wrote, 'it transpired that Holmes had been delayed on his way to the ground, and Leyland had opened the innings with Sutcliffe.'

Stevens had a better season, particularly with the bat, for he finished second to Hendren in the averages, but 17 behind, with Hearne in third place. Lee was having a series of seasons of moderate success, and Dales was not now scoring so well. Durston, Hearne and Haig continued to be the main wicket-takers year after year. Robins and Enthoven began playing championship cricket that year. Robins, who was still at school, began quietly with 77 runs in four innings and did not bowl. Nor did he do any better the next season, when his fielding, rather more than his batting, won him a Blue at Cambridge.

Also that year North took 34 wickets. He was one of a number of young professionals about that time who promised more than they actually achieved. There were others such as J. A. Powell, a googly bowler, who actually headed the county averages in 1926 by taking 28 wickets at 22.5. In the same season George Paine, a slow left-arm spinner, showed comparable promise in a few games. Archie Fowler and Beveridge were other bowlers, and Canning and Hart batsmen of whom much was expected. Later there were others, Andy Wilson, Watkins, Beton, Wignall, Nevell and Muncer.

It is very pleasant to have a large number of gifted amateurs on the books. It is, however, questionable if the best interests of the side are served by playing them automatically when they are available for only a handful of matches. There come times when none of them can turn out. Then the county suffers from having put the amateur before the professional. That several of the players mentioned would probably have made good, if properly encouraged in their early years at Lord's, is indicated by the experiences of those who got away. Paine went to qualify for Warwickshire. There he took 57 championship wickets in his first season, 75 in his second and 112 in his third. At the time Middlesex had become desperate for bowlers. His 75 wickets in 1930 were 14 more than the highest bag for Middlesex, who not surprisingly finished in sixteenth position.

Between the wars the Nursery at Lord's brought along numerous fine players for other counties some of whom Middlesex could have had in addition to those such as Paine, Wilson and Muncer, who actually played for Middlesex before leaving London. On the whole the rest of the country benefited probably as much as Middlesex from the Nursery at Lord's. Yorkshire did particularly well from the cricketing upbringing which Bowes had received at Lord's. The young professional in Middlesex needed luck no less than skill to establish himself in the county side, so long as admittance to amateurs remained easy.

In 1926 Middlesex fared badly in their matches with other members of the big six. Hobbs made his 316 not out without giving a chance in a Surrey innings of 579 for five wickets. He batted under seven hours and hit 41 fours. Jardine also scored a century. Hendren made his highest score, when they went in for a second time against Yorkshire at Lord's 165 runs down. His 213 were made out of a total of 367. The only success against one of the big six was the unexpected defeat of Nottinghamshire, who needed no more than 196 in the last innings in favourable conditions. Hearne turned on one of his finest bowling performances, which were now becoming less frequent. He took five wickets for 16 in 40 balls, and Notts were beaten by 75 runs.

On the whole it was the bowling which held Middlesex back, though Haig got through a tremendous amount of work, and Durston kept plugging away. He was now 32, a veteran age for fast bowlers, and in subsequent seasons he tended to bowl slow-medium off breaks more and more. The batting was as strong as ever. Though the Tests kept Hendren out of seven games, his aggregate of 1,639 in championship games was more than 500 more than any other batsman. Hearne averaged 55, Bruce nearly 39, Stevens 37 and Mann 36. Those figures did not include the match against the Australians, which was a triumph for Stevens and had much to do with his selection for the last two Tests. The Australians had made 489, Allen taking the last four wickets in 11 balls, and Middlesex were in danger of following on. Stevens, first in and ninth out, enabled them to escape. He scored the first century against the touring team, on the last day of May, and he batted five hours and 20 minutes for 149. When the eighth wicket fell, 75 were still needed. The trusty Murrell, then 45 and nearing the end of his fine career, helped him to add 76 and himself went on to make 54.

Mann's great match was at Edgbaston, when they were without Hendren, Hearne and Stevens. Seven amateurs with Lee, Murrell, Paine and Powell formed the team. Middlesex were so outplayed in the first innings that Warwickshire led by 206. Mann saved Middlesex by batting just over five hours for 194, and the match was drawn. That was a fortunate match for Paine, since he took five wickets for 77 and three for 25 and sufficiently impressed Warwickshire, for whom he shortly afterwards began to qualify by residence.

The points-scoring system in the county championship was undergoing considerable alteration in this period. That year five points were awarded for a win. In a drawn match three went to the first-innings leader and one to the other side. Those matches in which there was not a first-innings result were ignored

Above left, Joe Murrell, who won his place in the county side as a batsman before there was a vacancy as wicketkeeper
Above right, Harry Lee hitting a six to leg against Essex at Leyton
Below, the Hon. C. N. Bruce batting against Lancashire at Lord's

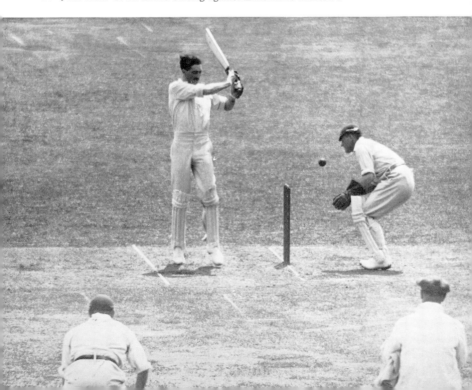

Frank Mann, Warner's successor
as captain, under whom
Middlesex won the championship
in his first year
Below, the match with Surrey at
Lord's which clinched the
championship for Middlesex,
showing part of the crowd who
filled the ground and caused the
gates to be closed. Warner is
batting, Hobbs fielding at cover
and Strudwick keeping wicket

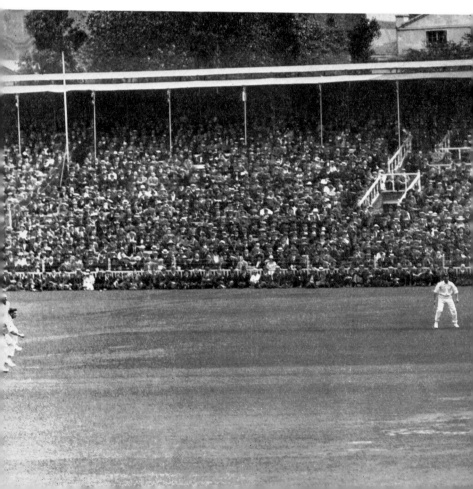

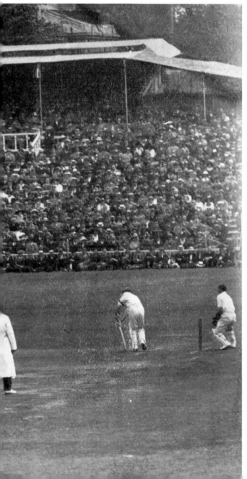

A match with Kent at Lord's in 1920. Skeet is caught at the wicket by Hubble off Tich Freeman

Nigel Haig, the captain who steered the county through their difficult times between the wars

The batsman's view of fast bowler Fred Durston

Reg Bettington, the county's third Australian all-rounder, bowling his leg breaks at the Oval

for percentage purposes. In 1927 a win counted eight, and in a drawn match the points were divided five and three. If there was no result in more than six hours of play each side took four. If there was under six hours of play without result the match did not count. Then in 1929 the percentage system was dropped, but only temporarily. Each county had to play 28 matches with eight points being given for a win, five and three in a drawn game and four each when no first-innings result was obtained. When the percentage system was revived in 1933, 15 points were awarded for a win.

The game was becoming governed by safety-first considerations. Pitches were easy, scoring was high, and first-innings points were playing too great a part in deciding the championship. As happened in the comparable period after the Second World War, when play became negative, the legislators were busy. Happily between the wars they occupied themselves mainly with fiddling about with the championship scoring system.

Only two important law changes were made. The first came in 1928, when the stumps were enlarged. The change was made 26 years after it had first been suggested by a meeting of county captains at Lord's in 1902 that the wicket should be increased from eight inches wide to nine. At the same time an experiment was tried by which a batsman could be out lbw even though he might have snicked the ball on to his pad. That was not likely to be a great success, and the next change, which allowed lbw decisions to balls pitched outside the off-stump, has been widely criticised as responsible for many of the ills to which the game subsequently succumbed.

The enlarging of the wicket was overdue – not that the bigger ones did much to check high scoring. Nor did the change lead to more positive play. It was in fact made before the safety-first cricket became noticeable in the early thirties. If the legislators of the fifties and sixties had heeded history, they would not have tampered to such a harmful extent with so many laws. They would have appreciated that legislation does not cure such ills. It was much criticism in the thirties and insistence by county committees on a more positive brand of cricket that brought about the improvement. The cricket played in the last two or three seasons before the war was enterprising and attractive enough for the most critical.

There was plenty of high scoring and many drawn games in 1927, although July and August were unpleasantly wet. Middlesex drew 14 of their 24 championship games, and they did not have a single win in their last 13 games during the wet months. They slipped one more place to ninth. Hearne was able to play throughout, but Durston was handicapped by a strain, Allen dropped out before the end of June, Stevens played only five times and Bruce not at all. Moreover, Dales played only two games and had just about come to the end of his period of success. Killick and Robins were disappointing. Murrell gave way to Fred Price, who kept wicket excellently but was not then out of the rabbit stage with the bat. The improvement there was yet to come and when it did it landed him in the number seven batting position when he played his only Test against Australia in 1938.

Hendren was again far ahead of all other Middlesex batsmen; with his aggregate of 2,784 and average 73.26 he was fourth in the national averages. He had some great bursts of scoring. In June he had innings of 101, 50, and 201 not out. In July he hit 150 for the Players, then 127, 62 not out and 140, and at the end of the season he scored two centuries for M C C against Kent. He made eight of the 15 centuries hit for Middlesex in the championship and 13 altogether. Hearne started the season in such form that he made 750 in May, and they included an innings of 245 not out against Gloucestershire at Bristol. Then he fell off, but he had a match of great all-round success when Middlesex concluded their programme against Surrey at Lord's. In the first Surrey innings he took eight wickets for 39, following this with an innings of 167 not out. Even with his fine play Surrey won comfortably by five wickets, having routed Middlesex for 54 in the first innings, of which Hendren made 22 and Enthoven 16.

Enthoven, a powerfully-built man with considerable driving powers, was criticized that season for playing too cautiously and hiding his attacking strokes. Once he did let himself go properly, when Middlesex were doing none too well in reply to a

Lancashire total of 413 at Lord's. Indeed with eight wickets down they still needed 55 to avoid having to follow on. Enthoven had studiously taken 145 minutes to reach 50. Then he proceeded to play his natural game. In particular he attacked the fast bowling of Macdonald, who that season took 150 wickets. His stroke play was so brilliant that he hit 89 more in 55 minutes.

Middlesex, as ever, were unpredictable. They defeated Yorkshire and yet fell to Worcestershire, who did not succeed in beating any other side. Haig's swing bowling, seven wickets for 33, which put Yorkshire out for 81 on the first day, and finally Hendren's not-out innings of 68 gave them a six-wicket win. At Worcester they were twice rattled out by Fred Root, who bowled in-swingers at medium-quick pace to a leg field and also made the odd ball straighten, or even move back from leg on pitching. The batsman could not regard him solely as an in-swing bowler and shape his play accordingly. That day he had five wickets in each innings at a total cost of 80, and Worcestershire gained their only win with six wickets to spare.

Although they suffered five defeats by an innings, at the hands of Lancashire, Kent, Yorkshire, Gloucestershire and Hampshire, Middlesex rose one place in 1928. They did so in spite of having again to do without Hearne for much of the season, and in spite of Allen's playing only twice and Stevens not at all. To offset such handicaps Hendren had his greatest batting year, Lee came right back to top form, and Bettington played one season, or a large portion of it, before returning to Australia. His 54 wickets were perhaps more important than the 605 runs he scored. Lee had been running an average in the 20s for season after season. Now he suddenly spurted to 42 with a total of 1,602.

That was a season of vast scoring, in which Hendren played a large part, for his 3,311 was his largest aggregate. Though his average was over 70, he was only fourth in the national list. Three other batsmen exceeded 3,000, Ernest Tyldesley, Sutcliffe and Mead. Centuries were scored galore. Hendren, Mead and Sutcliffe each had 13, Hobbs and Woolley 12 each. No wonder it was thought necessary to enlarge the wicket! For Middlesex Hendren hit 11 centuries and made 2,471 runs in the 24 championship games.

Hearne's misfortunes continued with injury in the match against the West Indies. He was then threatening to rival the scoring feats of Hendren, for in eight championship games he was averaging nearly 76 and had scored 682. He suffered the injury which put him out for the rest of the season when fielding a fierce drive by Learie Constantine. That Middlesex lost that match was entirely due to this meteoric cricket of Constantine, fast bowler and hitter extraordinary. He did nothing of note while Middlesex were scoring 352 for six wickets declared, with Haig 119 and Hendren 100 not out. Constantine's one wicket cost 77. He batted number seven, and, when he went in, the West Indies were 79 for five. Inside the next hour he hit 86 out of 107. In their second innings Middlesex made 136, Constantine took seven wickets for 57, and only Hendren, who made 52, played him with any success. Yet Middlesex still looked like winning until Constantine went in at 121 for five to play in precisely the same way again. He hammered the Middlesex bowling to score at the same hectic pace, and with two sixes and 12 fours he made 103 of the next 136.

Durston had a good bowling season, taking more than 100 wickets, yet Middlesex had to field through some long innings that batsman's summer. On three occasions three opposing batsmen made centuries against them in the same innings. Holmes, Oldroyd and Mitchell did so in a Yorkshire total of 479; Kennedy, Mead and Hosie in Hampshire's 540; and Bowley, Duleepsinhji and Tate in the 496 of Sussex. On the last-named occasion Haig won the toss and sent in Sussex, when the game started late after rain. They hit their 496 in six hours and a half. The reply, even if it took 105 minutes longer, was more than satisfactory: 497 for seven wickets. Killick, 140, and Hendren, 158, stayed together for five hours and shared a stand of 301. The same pair scored centuries against Surrey at the Oval, where they put on 195 together. Another outsize total against them was Kent's 539 for nine, but they themselves also ran up tall scores, including a particularly pleasing total of 488 against Yorkshire at Leeds.

Haig took over the captaincy from Mann that year. The added responsibility seemed only to benefit him in his own play. He was already doing more than one man's share. Since Lee was now without a regular opening partner, Haig often went in first with him and also opened the bowling. Now he had the captaincy as well. He had a good season in 1928 and the best of his career in the following year. He had done the double twice before without much to spare. In 1929 he left both targets far behind, for he made 1,552 runs and took 129 wickets.

The pressing need had been for new bowlers to ease the strain on Durston, Hearne and Haig. Now they appeared. Peebles had played briefly during the previous season and taken six wickets for 129; Robins had been turning his attention to leg-spin. Now both arrived with a bang, and Middlesex enjoyed the unusual experience of having three amateur bowlers each taking 100 wickets. Peebles took the lead, his wickets costing under 20 runs each, but Robins and Haig were not far behind. Their bags in championship cricket were Peebles 107, Robins 125 and Haig 100. In all cricket they dismissed 383 batsmen. A fourth amateur, Allen, played little but made his mark by taking all ten Sussex wickets in an innings at Lord's for 40, and by playing an innings of 155 against Surrey at the Oval.

By his standards Hendren had a moderate season both for the county and for England against South Africa. He lost his Test place after the fourth match. Killick, who was still at Cambridge, played in two of the Tests, in which he made 81 in four innings. Robins had greater success in his one match, for, though he failed with the bat, he took five wickets for 79. Although Hendren's aggregate for Middlesex dropped to 1,363 and in all first-class games to 2,213 with only five centuries, his 38.94 gave him first place yet again for Middlesex. Hearne was close on his heels, thanks largely to his 285 not out against Essex at Leyton, which at the time was the county's highest score.

Even with less than usual from Hendren the batting was strong and could shrug off the absence of Stevens and, except in one championship match, of Killick. Lee had another fine season, almost 2,000 in all matches, and Robins exceeded 1,000, of which 871 were scored in the championship, to do the double for the only time in his career. That he did not continue doing so was doubtless a result of his dropping out for some years, while he was employed by, and playing cricket for, Sir Julian Cahn. The latter gathered together a team of first-class players in Nottingham and had a long fixture list to occupy his troops. Add Haig's considerable batting contribution and, with valuable innings by such amateurs as Guise, Newman and Bertie Carris of the Cambridge side, Middlesex were not often short of runs.

They made their highest total at the Oval, where Lee made 225 and Allen followed with his 155. From 514 for five wickets declared they proceeded to beat Surrey by an innings, despite an innings of 97 on the last day by Hobbs. Peebles had earlier taken six wickets for 26. A good example of Haig's spirited cricket as opening batsman and opening bowler was in the match with Worcestershire at Lord's. He made 130, sharing an opening stand of 175 in 135 minutes with Lee, and then helped to bowl Worcestershire to an innings defeat with four for 94 and three for 32.

Though Durston was handicapped by knee trouble, he took 75 wickets in all matches, and Hearne 61. Yet Middlesex finished no higher than sixth. Killick in his only championship game scored 71 against Nottinghamshire. He also played against the South Africans, but, though he played an innings of 111, the county lost by eight wickets.

Middlesex seemed to be set fair. They could expect to advance still further and soon challenge for the championship. Instead, everything went wrong, and they suffered their worst season. Peebles went up to Oxford and could not play until late in the season. Robins joined Cahn's circus and played only four championship games. The other leading amateurs were only occasionally available, and the side was continually subject to chop and change in what was for them the dismal summer of 1930. No fewer than 33 players turned out in the 28 matches. Only Haig, Lee and Price played in all of them. Hearne missed six games, and representative calls kept Hendren out of 11. He did not enjoy one of his best seasons, his aggregate falling below 2,000 for once, but he was somewhat harshly treated when dropped after two Tests. He had made two good scores against Australia, but the selection of teams that summer was not always realistic.

Robins was dropped at the same time, although he had been England's most likely bowler in the two matches.

The final placing was 16th, only three points clear of humble Northamptonshire at the bottom of the list. After three months bottom place seemed to be theirs for the taking. Their record was then: played 20, won 0, lost 7, drawn 13. The reappearance of Peebles and occasionally Allen brought much needed relief. Three of the last eight matches were won and two more lost. What Peebles meant to the side was clearly shown in the figures, for he finished all on his own at the top of the bowling averages. His 44 wickets cost only 10.9 each. Only Allen with 26 at 17.26 was anywhere near him. Third place was taken by Beveridge, slow left-arm spinner, who took 29 wickets at just over 20 each. Hearne, Durston and Haig were the main wicket-takers, but Haig's 53 were horribly expensive, his average being over 37.

For most of the season, until the late arrival of Peebles, the three veterans had to slog away with little relief. That Haig was slipping back was not surprising. He was then 42 and over-worked. Durston, who was bowling off-breaks more and more and using pace only with the new ball, was now making himself useful with the bat. His championship total was 619.

Though Hulme scored his first century, against Warwickshire at Edgbaston, there was no obvious sign yet of help for the old men from young professionals. That was not surprising, for they were not exactly handled sensibly. Canning, for instance, was in and out of the side, and when he did play he was moved up and down the order in a manner calculated to bewilder a young bats-man. For two matches he was the number three and scored 85 against Hampshire. In the next match against Sussex he was number ten, after which he was dropped. When he returned he rose suddenly from number nine to open the innings with Lee.

While the county were doing so badly in the first three months, it was galling to see some who had done so much in the previous season playing with success elsewhere. Peebles had a splendid season at Oxford, and both he and Robins played for the Gentle-men at Lord's. There they took 11 of the 13 wickets lost by the Players. Robins also did well in the Test trial. How Middlesex could have done with some of the wickets they were taking outside the county! That Paine, now with Warwickshire, took five of their wickets in an innings at Edgbaston was no less galling.

Hendren and Hearne headed the batsmen with averages in the early 40s, and Lee was the main supporter, though his average dropped to 26.6. Several of the amateurs, making fleeting appearances, did little with the bat. Enthoven had one fine game, making centuries in both innings against Sussex, for whom Duleepsinhji also made two in the same match. Otherwise he did comparatively little in his nine appearances. Newman also played nine times, and his aggregate of 381 owed much to a couple of hundreds against Warwickshire and Essex. Allen's batting failed him.

Outside the championship, four other games were played, and all four were lost. Because they did not meet Surrey in the championship they had two non-competitive friendlies. Friendship was not obvious, for Surrey walloped them by an innings and 177 runs at the Oval and by nine wickets at Lord's. Middlesex lost also to Cambridge and the Australians. The end of a wet summer was a relief for Haig and his toilers.

The next summer was also wet. In the championship 91 playing days were totally washed out, and 20 more in other first-class matches. When the rain did hold off, the weather was so often cheerless that gates suffered. Two such seasons in succession hit county treasuries hard. In 1931 the 17 collectively were in the region of £20,000 in the red on the year's working. Middlesex lost £1,347, but they had assets of over £15,000 and were not greatly concerned. Others were less fortunate. Because they had to play 28 championship games, more than the local demand for such cricket could meet in some centres, the system was changed yet again. A minimum of 24 matches was agreed for 1932, and the percentage system was restored.

Middlesex improved to eleventh place in 1931, winning five times against three the previous year. Most of the good work was done in the first month with a predominantly professional side. They had four wins in their first six encounters, and in that time also defeated the touring New Zealanders. Peebles had ended his stay at Oxford in order to tour South Africa with M C C. He

Above, Grenville Stevens, all-rounder who played for Middlesex and for the Gentlemen against the Players at Lord's while still at school *Right*, Fred Price, Murrell's successor behind the wicket

Ian Peebles bowling against Gloucestershire at Lord's, J. W. Hearne the fielder at mid-on and Hendren on the off side

Robins, the adventurer, nearly half-way down the pitch to tackle Grimmett when Middlesex met the Australians in 1934. He deflected the ball wide of Oldfield at the wicket, escaped being dismissed and went on to 65 during a stand of 142 with Hendren

was regularly available and started the season in tremendous form. He had 11 for 130 against Glamorgan, then 11 for 124 against Essex and ten for 107 against Somerset. Hearne with the bat was also off to a flying start with centuries in each innings against Glamorgan, whom they were meeting for the first time. He next made 83 and 38 against Gloucestershire, but his health subsequently troubled him yet again.

After that fine start the season became no better than the previous one. Not another win was gained until the final match against Northamptonshire, who were bottom of the table by a very wide margin. In the meantime they had been dismissed for under 200 14 times, while themselves bowling out opponents similarly only five times. Amateurs came and went once more, but, in addition to Peebles, Stevens was able to play in 20 matches. He batted well, making three centuries and taking third place to Hendren and Hearne in the averages, but his bowling was expensive. Enthoven played ten times with modest success, Killick once only, and then he scored 206 against Warwickshire at Lord's.

With Hendren resuming his conquering batting ways there should have been no worry about the batting. However, there was a wide gap between Hendren and the others. He made 2,122 and averaged over 60 in the championship. Hearne and Stevens, with just over 32, and Lee, with just over 30, were next in the list. After them there was another considerable gap. Hulme was playing quite regularly but not yet making much progress. Sims, who first played in 1930, was now said to be showing promise as a batsman.

Although his leg break was even then beginning to desert him, Peebles was the leading wicket-taker. He had 100 at 17.35 – 139 in all matches – and Durston, becoming more proficient at off-break bowling, increased his bag in competitive games to 70 and reduced the cost of his wickets. Allen strengthened the attack in his few appearances, but Hearne, Stevens and Haig bought their wickets in a dear market. Robins played in only two matches.

Hendren that year took a second Benefit during the Sussex match at Lord's and enlivened it by scoring a century. Hearne had made his two centuries in a match, the only time in his career, and later Hendren also had two in a match against Warwickshire at Edgbaston. This was for the second time, but the first for the county. In subsequent years he made hundreds in each innings twice more, in 1933 against Kent and 1936, when he was aged 47, against Surrey. Both events took place at Lord's, where a high proportion of his most memorable innings were played.

The year 1932 was almost a replica of 1931. Again they began well by winning four of the first ten matches, but in the rest of the season they won only twice more. With nine defeats they again finished eleventh. Two veterans, Hearne and Durston, enjoyed Indian summers. Hearne, like Hendren, scored more than 2,000 runs in all first-class games, and Durston took more than 100 championship wickets. Peebles, however, played in only 16 matches, in which he took 72 wickets, Robins in five and Allen in four, while Stevens, turning out 13 times, had very ordinary figures, and Enthoven fared badly.

The bowling indeed was the cause of their humble position. Haig soldiered on, but he was achieving less and less. Again he played in all 28 matches, but his runs totalled no more than 552 and his wickets 33. This was his last year of captaincy on his own. He could not spare time to play regularly in the future. During the next two seasons he shared the captaincy with Enthoven, who played in the first half of the season and then handed over to Haig. After 1934 Haig retired. He came to the captaincy at a bad time, and he had no real chance of making a reputation in that field. The most he could do was to keep the county going through the bad period. He did that in whole-hearted fashion. No captain surely ever worked harder for his side as opening batsman, opening bowler and skipper, even when he was advancing well into his forties. A stout heart and great stamina were needed to toil and persevere as Haig did.

After Durston and Peebles, Sims was the next wicket-taker with 41. He had started to develop his leg break bowling, and he improved also his batting figures. Near the end of the season he scored a century in a remarkable match with Surrey at the Oval, which stepped up his aggregate to 639 and his average above 20. Hulme also made a leap forward by exceeding 1,000 for the first time and scoring two centuries, and he moved above Lee in the averages. So, although Hendren was kept out of the early matches by injury, Middlesex scored heavily throughout. Unfortunately for them their opponents did the same.

The highest total came after Leicestershire had declared at 479 for six wickets. Lee, Hearne and Hendren scored hundreds, and the innings brought them 573. Totals of 421 against Kent, with another hundred by Hearne, and 455 at the Oval were other fine performances. The Oval total also followed a mammoth innings by their opponents. Middlesex were out for 141 at the first attempt, and Surrey built up a vast lead before declaring at 540 for nine. Hobbs made 92, Jardine 126 and Freddie Brown 212. Brown massacred the bowling. He clouted seven sixes and scored above a run a minute. With Jardine he shared a stand of 143 in 85 minutes, and the innings was brought to a tumultuous conclusion as he and Maurice Allom put on 155 in 65 minutes for the ninth wicket. Allom's share was 57. The Middlesex retort was 455. Sims, opening the innings, batted four hours and forty minutes for 103, and Hendren made 145.

Towards the end only 20 minutes remained, and Surrey needed 57. They got them, losing four wickets on the way, off the last possible ball with the clock already showing closing time. When Jardine faced the last three balls from Durston, ten were still needed. Off the first of them he was missed by Enthoven at deep mid-off and ran two. The next ball, which was overpitched and well wide of the off stump, was chopped through the slips for four, and Jardine completed the astonishing match with a drive straight to the pavilion boundary.

Surrey also won the more prosaic return match at Lord's by 229 runs. Brown was again in great form. In the first Surrey innings he hit 135 in just over two hours, and in the second, when Hobbs made a century, he was 35 not out at the declaration. In the field he took six Middlesex wickets for 63 and two more in the second innings.

Divided captaincy invariably is unsuccessful. Positions at 12th and 10th place in the seasons shared by Haig and Enthoven were as much as they might hope for. The first season was dominated by Hendren, who for the third time exceeded 3,000 in all first-class matches. He made 2,479 of them in the championship. There he accounted for eight of the 14 centuries scored for the county, and with 63.56 he headed the averages by a margin of 28. Hearne was next with 35 and Hulme third with nearly 24.

In addition to his two centuries against Kent at Lord's, and his highest-ever 301 not out, made in seven hours, against Worcestershire at Dudley, Hendren made the season personally memorable by also scoring 1,110 in August. He further shone with scores of eight and 152 not out and 55 and 111 while Middlesex were being beaten twice in ten days by Surrey. Yorkshire also walloped them twice by ten wickets, for the bowling of Bowes, Verity and Macaulay was too much for them.

If 14 matches were lost against the seven won, there were some encouraging signs. Price had so far developed his batting that he was used as an opener in several matches. His aggregate of 818, average 21.5, represented a distinct advance. Then late in the season the county once more introduced a boy straight from the school side. He was opening bowler, Peter Judge, of St Paul's. In fact Judge did not develop as expected with Middlesex, and later he moved to Glamorganshire. His potential was clear, but he did not school himself to realize it. So Sims, who had 52 wickets that season, remained as the main hope of bowling reinforcement from within the club. That was an urgent need, for the largest bag in the championship was Hearne's 53. Peebles without his once-so-dangerous leg break was now more expensive, his 45 victims costing 22 runs each.

The committee had had the idea of encouraging more club players and sought closer co-operation with the clubs. The need was a settled side, and unless they could find ready-made club players willing to take up cricket as a regular occupation, there was no likelihood of future gain from the idea. Casual amateurs coming into a county side now and then merely disrupt the regulars. Year after year at this time the county used about 30 different players. Yorkshire, champions in 1933, fielded no more than 19, and eleven of them played in 22 matches or more. The other eight merely plugged a gap when one of the regulars was missing by reason of Test duty, injury or, in the case of Bowes, because he was still on call to M C C.

If Sims, recovering from an operation for appendicitis, did not advance rapidly in 1934, the arrival of Jim Smith from Wiltshire made a vast difference. In his first season he took 139 championship wickets, 172 in all, and was sixth in the national averages. Number one in that list with 156 wickets was the man Middlesex allowed to slip away, George Paine!

Smith's arrival enabled Durston to go into honourable retirement. Lee also was easing out of the side and played in only four championship games. He was going out on a high note, for at Edgbaston he scored his final century. That was a summer of generally firm pitches, which suited the new fast bowler. He had the height to get lift from such pitches, and he made full use of it. His big hitting was also welcome, and among the hits for six he made in his first season was one that shattered the window of the committee room at Lord's. He was so successful that he was chosen for the Players against the Gentlemen at Lord's after little more than two months in the first-class game.

Two older members made striking advances. Hulme not only exceeded his best previous batting figures by nearly 500 and scored four centuries, but he so improved his medium-paced bowling that he took 27 wickets at reasonable cost. In the previous season the cost of his six victims had been 61 each. Although he missed five championship matches, Hulme made the most runs with 1,258, though his average was nearly seven below Hendren's 43.77. The other batting gain was Price, who was the only other man to score more than 1,000 in championship games. He went in first with Hart, who was himself not far from the 1,000. Middlesex had suffered from the lack of a regular opening pair. If these two were not the final answer to the problem, they did become regulars that season, and the first four in the batting order, with Hearne and Hendren following, could be stabilized.

Hendren again missed several matches while playing Test cricket. He played in four of the matches against Australia, hitting a century at Old Trafford, and missed the fifth only because he was slightly injured. Peebles played only in the early part of the season, when he was more successful than in 1933. Allen also bowled well in the few matches he could play, and Robins began to come into the picture again in preparation for taking over the captaincy in 1935. He was in good form both with bat and ball.

What a difference there might have been if he had continued to play regularly after the great season in which the three amateurs each took more than 100 wickets. Quite apart from the runs he made and the wickets he took, the zest with which he played cricket was a tonic for the other players. He was a cricketer who did not understand the meaning of safety first. It was foreign to his nature.

It was while he was skipper that he fell victim of Patsy Hendren's leg-pulling. They were batting together at Lord's, Robins with the strike at the nursery end. He went far down the pitch, missed and was so sure that he must be stumped that he began to walk on down the pitch towards the pavilion without looking behind. Until Patsy suddenly shouted: 'Look out, skipper!' Robins turned and dived full length for his crease. When he picked himself up, covered in dust, it was to discover that he had indeed been stumped cleanly, and long before he made his abortive dive. When he passed the far wicket, Hendren was leaning on his bat, an innocent expression on his puckish face. 'Bad luck. skipper,' he murmured.

7 Championship Challenges Again, 1936-9

One era was ending and another beginning. Haig had endured, always cheerfully, the frustration of seeing the county through the bleak final years of the old one. Robins was taking over when the much-needed, new players were beginning to make their presence felt. He was ideally equipped to bring them along.

The two eras were linked by Hendren, who looked like going on for ever, reeling off 2,000 and more a season in all first-class games. Hearne, then 45, managed one more fairly full season, but his top score was 57, his average down to little more than 18, and he took only 16 wickets. After one game in the following year he dropped out altogether. Considering his health troubles, it was remarkable that he did so well for so long. There is no saying what he might have achieved given good health.

Whereas Haig may be said to have taken over the control of the county in autumn, Robins began in spring. With himself and Peebles as leading spinners and Smith one of the best fast bowlers in the country, he had a strong bowling nucleus. When Allen was also available, the opening attack was formidable indeed. In his first year, moreover, the bowling strength was greatly increased when Sims broke into the front rank. He was actually the only member of the attack to take more than 100 wickets in championship matches, though Smith also did so in all matches.

The batting, hinged on Hendren, was also not calculated to cause him headaches. Though Hulme suffered a set-back in 1935, which was followed by a swift revival the following year, there were to be two notable recruits. John Human and Owen-Smith, an all-round cricketer whose inclinations and temperament precisely matched those of the skipper, came into the side. Muncer,

too, played that year and batted usefully, while Price and Hart
continued to act as the openers with reasonable results. In the
background there were two other formidable recruits. While
qualifying for the county Bill Edrich scored three centuries in nine
matches for MCC during 1936. Meanwhile in 1935 Middlesex
entered the minor counties championship for the first time. They
carried off the title, and in their ranks for a couple of matches was
Denis Compton. Jack Robertson and Jack Young also played.

Runs were not easily made at Lord's in those years. The
ground had been ravaged by leather-jackets, and the pitch was
by no means trustworthy. In particular the ball left it at variable
and unpredictable heights, and it generally favoured the spin
bowlers. The true value of Smith was, accordingly, appreciated
more away from Lord's. The damage done by the leather-jackets
could not stop Hendren's scoring, nor could persistent knee
trouble, once he recovered from a bad start. In his first seven
innings on the ground he made only 66. From then until the end
of the season his average in championship games was almost 70.
His part in lifting the county to third position behind Yorkshire
and Derbyshire was 1,649 runs and an average of 51.5. He
made more than twice as many runs as any other Middlesex
batsman. His average was more than double that of Owen-Smith,
who was in second place.

Lancashire were twice beaten. The spin of Sims, Robins and
Peebles overcame them at Lord's, and at Old Trafford the pace
of Allen, who took ten wickets for 74 in the two innings, and
Smith was too much for them. They themselves suffered defeat
by an innings at Leeds, where Yorkshire had the better of the
conditions and Verity took 11 wickets. Rather surprisingly they
were twice beaten by Warwickshire, for whom Paine took ten
wickets in the two games. But they had 11 wins to set against five
losses. Robins played his full part, and his 60 championship
wickets were economically taken at 17 runs each. Sims was consistently successful, and he finished with a splendid match against
Surrey at Lord's. His scores were 53 and 25 not out, his bowling
five wickets for 42 and four for 55. Rain, however, prevented
Middlesex from winning, and both Surrey games were left
drawn.

Human played in 24 matches. He was below his best form at first, but late in the season he played successive innings of 144 at the Oval and 127 at Trent Bridge. Ten players appeared in 19 or more matches, and the number of men used dropped to 20. The benefit of being able to keep a side together was reflected in the much improved results. Towards the end of August another who was shortly to become a regular, Laurie Gray, came into the side and had striking success immediately by taking two wickets for 17 and six for 32, while helping to defeat Kent by an innings.

Robins that year returned to the Test side against the South Africans, and he scored a century in the fourth match at Old Trafford. Sims also represented England, and both were due for inclusion in the next team to tour Australia under Allen. Peebles was no longer in the running for the England side. His leg-break had deserted him, and he was now making less and less impression with the unsupported googly. He played only in the early part of the season, and, though his 22 wickets were taken at a cost of below 20, he was not now a match-winner.

Allen played only twice that year, but in 1936 he tuned up for Australia in nine championship games and was in sterling form. For the first time since before the war Hendren was displaced at the top of the county averages. With a top score of 137 against Worcestershire Allen averaged 50.66 and pipped Hendren by nearly three runs. Nevertheless, Hendren was as masterful as ever. He made 1,963 in championship matches. His season's aggregate was 2,654, considerably more than that of any other batsman that year, and he was third in the averages – fourth if Edrich, who played only nine innings, is included.

Third to Allen and Hendren was Compton in his first highly auspicious season, a decidedly damp one and not on that account ideal for a young newcomer. Hulme jumped back to form. He again hit four centuries in the championship and exceeded 1,000. Robins, Hart and Sims made valuable scores, and Smith on occasions again hit joyfully. Among the occasional amateurs at this period, in addition to Enthoven and Newman, were: W. H. Webster, M. Tindall, F. E. Covington and R. E. C. Butterworth. Webster made a century against Gloucestershire at Bristol.

Ten wins against four defeats were not quite enough to win the championship, but on two or three occasions rain stopped them when they were on the point of winning. Yet, their bad luck with the weather was nothing compared with Yorkshire's. Rain interfered so much, particularly during their home games, that 18 of their 30 were left drawn. They had little or no chance of retaining the championship. Derbyshire seized the opportunity to win it for the first, and so far, only time by virtue of their powerful bowling. This was so strong with Copson, Alfred Pope, Mitchell and Armstrong that they won even without George Pope, who suffered cartilage trouble in a knee early in the season.

Defeats by small margins in their opening two matches against Warwickshire and Esssex were not an auspicious start for Middlesex. Subsequently, however, in addition to the ten championship wins they also overcame the Indian touring team. At Scarborough they failed badly against the bowling of Smailes and Bowes. They were all out for 127 and reached that modest figure only because Smith hit 56 of the last 57. He hit four sixes and three times sent the ball out of the ground. After Sutcliffe had made 202 and Leyland 107, Yorkshire bowled on a worn pitch and won by an innings. The other defeat was at Lord's when they fielded badly, and their batting broke down against Lancashire.

The only obvious weakness lay in the opening batsmen. Hart did reasonably well, but Price was not cut out to go in first. He had worked hard in that position, but now it was becoming too much for him. His average was under 16 and his top score 45 not out. Otherwise there was not much wrong with the batting. Hendren was the first man in the country to reach 1,000 and then 2,000, and he finished the championship season by scoring a century in each innings against Surrey at Lord's. That was again a happy match for Sims, whose total bag was ten wickets for 106. During the previous winter he had been on tour through Australia and New Zealand with Errol Holmes's predominantly amateur side. He was much the most successful bowler and took 70 wickets in the first-class matches. Tests were not played.

He and Smith were the leading bowlers again, well supported by Robins and Gray and, in nine matches, by Allen. The last-named had a particularly good match against Worcestershire at Lord's. He played an innings of 137 and altogether took seven wickets for 74. Among numerous good returns by Smith was his 12 wickets for 59 against Essex at Colchester. His most memorable innings was played at Lord's against Somerset, when he clouted 69 including two sixes and ten fours in 26 minutes. Peebles played in 13 championship games, but his 25 wickets cost 23.6 each.

Having climbed to second place, Middlesex held it for the next three seasons before the war. The first of them, 1937, was Hendren's last. He went out while still at the top to become the coach at Harrow School. His age may have been 48, but he was still an agile fielder, and there was no noticeable loss of batting skill. He made 1,809 runs in his final season, and only Edrich exceeded his 1,380 in their championship games. Of his five centuries the fifth was made in his last match at Lord's against the ancient rivals from the Oval. That he made a duck in the second innings, a sentimental occasion with everyone, including his opponents, applauding him all the way to the wicket, was in keeping with such events. Similar salutations of great players, when coming to play their last innings, were too much for Hobbs and Bradman at the end of their Test careers. Hobbs at the Oval in 1930 did manage nine runs in his final innings against Australia. Bradman on the same ground 18 years later was bowled for a duck by Eric Hollies.

For Middlesex Hendren made 40,302 runs and hit 119 centuries. It is safe to say that both will always remain in the books as the county records. With so many fewer first-class matches being played in the seventies, and no likelihood of the numbers being materially increased, those figures are out of reach of modern players.

Middlesex that year were a very fine county side. Hendren, Compton and Edrich were the foundation of their batting strength. Smith, Sims, Robins, Gray and, for nearly half their matches, Owen-Smith, gave them a really dangerous attack, and the fielding was first class. Robins captained England against New Zealand, and when he was away Human led the side.

Compton strode forward. In his second season he was only

20 short of 2,000 in all matches. Though he had only three centuries, he averaged 47.14. Only nine batsmen, headed by Hammond, whose aggregate was 3,252, were in front of him in the national averages. Edrich, who exceeded 2,000 in his first season, also with three centuries, was 14th in the same list. But for Human's having to declare the innings against Worcestershire Compton might have won the Lawrence Trophy for the season's fastest hundred. He had made 80 in 43 minutes at the declaration, scoring faster at that point than Ames, who won the trophy with his 100 in 68 minutes for an England XI against the Indians.

The difference between Yorkshire, the champions, and Middlesex was the starts they made. Yorkshire began winning at once. Middlesex lost two of their first three matches and were behind on first innings in the other. At the season's end Yorkshire's percentage was 71.90 and that of Middlesex 68.33.

Middlesex had lost also to Lancashire and Nottinghamshire by the middle of June. After that they won 12 of the next 14, and drew the others, before winding up the season with unfinished games against Notts and Surrey. They were somewhat unlucky to lose to Lancashire at Lord's, for they batted last on a rain-affected pitch, and even so were beaten by only 22. That match was none the less a triumph for one Middlesex player, for Edrich made 175, his first century for the county, and 73 not out. The latter was a great innings on such a pitch, but of the other batsmen only Robins with 18 and Smith, 33, reached double figures. Smith hit 19 off one over from the fast-medium bowling of Pollard and clouted one ball over Father Time on top of the Grand Stand. Notts owed their win largely to the fast bowling of Bill Voce, who took six wickets for 41 and four for 36.

Once Middlesex had started on their successful run they won most matches by wide margins. Northamptonshire, Kent, Worcestershire, Sussex and Somerset, twice, went down by an innings. Moreover, before the successful run began they had already beaten Yorkshire in two days by an innings at Lord's, where Smith took ten wickets. In the return match, which was cut short by rain, Middlesex won first-innings points. His side's showing against the champions led Robins to issue a challenge to

Yorkshire. The latter accepted, and instead of the usual Champion County *v* The Rest a challenge match was played at the Oval. The challengers were put properly in their place. They did have the worst of the conditions, but defeat by an innings and 115 runs cannot on that account be explained away. Hutton scored 121, Verity took two wickets for 51 and eight for 43, and it was nearly all Yorkshire. A fine innings of 77 by Owen-Smith in a first-innings total of 185 was about all Middlesex salvaged from the wreck. The presence of Compton, who was by then on his footballing duties, could not have made good the difference between the two sides.

There was no challenge when the two counties finished in the same positions in 1938. County cricket had emerged from its dull, safety-first period. Of the 238 matches in the championship 162 reached definite results. Since no fewer than 47 days were entirely lost to wet weather, the total of 76 draws was surprisingly low. Yorkshire won 20 and lost two of their 28 games; Middlesex, winning 15 and losing 5, drew only twice.

The course of Middlesex was not as smooth as in the previous year. Compton and Edrich played in all the Tests against Australia and missed numerous county games. In the Tests Compton was much the more successful. For Middlesex Edrich was the major scorer. His 1,675 with an average of 64.42 was comparable to anything Hendren had been in the habit of accomplishing. Compton, second in the list, averaged just under 50. They were the only two who passed the 1,000 mark in the championship.

Two other newcomers, however, had very promising seasons. Sid Brown was the first young batsman to be tried as Edrich's opening partner. He scored his first century against Lancashire at Old Trafford, and he gave ample promise for the future. Much more impressive, however, was the start made by Jack Robertson, who came into the side for the Whitsun match with Sussex at Lord's early in June. He went in first with Edrich, and together they gave the side a brisk start during an opening stand of 129, which led to a total of 577 in the day. I can still see Robertson, playing with the elegance of Hearne, as he fully kept pace with Edrich. His off-driving in an innings of 81 was delightful, and his entire game was highly impressive. There can have been no more confident innings played by a man in his first match. He went on to take third place, among those who played upwards of ten innings, to Edrich and Compton with an average of nearly 33, and that with a highest score of 91.

That Sussex match, which was won by ten wickets, was the one in which Smith slammed his 69 in the last 20 minutes of the day and peppered passers-by in the St Johns Wood Road. Robins also went at a fine pace while making 137, and he also took six first-innings wickets.

The entrance of new opening batsmen freed Price, and his batting was revived by being used in lower positions. He, Robins, Hulme and Allen all averaged between 28 and 25, but it was mainly the batting which made the season a hard struggle when Edrich and Compton were missing. Another factor was the comparative lack of success of Sims. He was plagued by minor injuries. His scoring of runs was negligible, and his 47 wickets cost 30 each. However, a return to something approaching his early form by Peebles, who played enough to head the bowling figures with 32 wickets at 17.18, and the continued improvement of Gray did much to cover the temporary decline of Sims. Gray took 66 wickets, Robins 61 and Smith 107. Middlesex had no bowling worries in the championship, and as yet they had little need of Edrich's vigorous fast bowling. Indeed he bowled proportionally more in the Tests than he did in the championship.

The Gloucestershire matches produced unusual cricket. The encounter at Bristol was the one in which Smith hit his 8 sixes on the way to 66 in 18 minutes after Edrich and Hulme had scored centuries. Middlesex made 573 and won by an innings. At Lord's Middlesex won again after a second-innings declaration by Gloucestershire. The odd feature of the game was a tie at 478 in the first innings. Hammond, Neale and Andy Wilson, who not long before had been at Lord's with Middlesex, made centuries in the first knock. Edrich and Compton, scoring 182 and 163 respectively, replied with a stand of 304. Edrich, moreover, took the lead in the final innings with a quick-fire 71 as Middlesex hit 244 for seven wickets in 127 minutes to win.

That game was played in the middle of May. Soon afterwards Edrich hit 245 in a total of 474 against Nottinghamshire, which took his total to 981. He had six playing days in which to make 19 and join the select band who have scored 1,000 before the end of May. Against Worcestershire, who were beaten by an innings, he did not score in his only innings. The last match of the month was against the Australians, played on a rain-damaged pitch after the loss of a whole day's play. The Australians were out for 132, Middlesex for 188, of which Edrich managed only nine. So little time remained for play that his chance seemed to have gone. However, Bradman, who had passed 1,000 before that game, declared when his side was 58 ahead to give Edrich a chance of emulating him. There was time for six overs, and Edrich made 20 not out.

A costly match that year, which complicated the task of the Test selectors, was against Yorkshire. Again the pitch was damaged by rain. When Robins put Yorkshire in first, the ball flew alarmingly and unpredictably. Smith and Gray were menacing opponents, Hutton suffered a broken finger, Leyland a broken thumb, and Gibb a severe head wound. Paul Gibb was to have kept wicket in that match, while Arthur Wood stood down, in preparation for the approaching Test at Leeds. Ames at the time was out of commission, nursing a back injury, and Gibb was his reserve, though normally he played solely as a batsman for Yorkshire. None of the wounded Yorkshiremen could play in the Test, and England suffered their one defeat of the series. Price was the wicket-keeper in place of Gibb. They drew level in the historic final match at the Oval, where Hutton made 364 and Leyland 187, and together they shared a stand of 382.

With three men unable to bat in the second innings Yorkshire lost at Lord's. Their only other defeat was by Surrey at the Oval, where they were without half their regular players. They beat Middlesex into second place because they were better equipped to cover the absence of Test players. At different times Hutton, Leyland, Gibb, Bowes, Smailes, Verity and Wood were chosen for England. Middlesex lost only Compton, Edrich and, during one Test, Price. Instead of repeating his challenge of 1937 Robins wrote to Brian Sellers, the Yorkshire captain, admitting that 'your side is too good for us.'

Robins now resigned the captaincy. Business in the City

demanded his attention, and he was succeeded by Peebles. He, too, proved a good leader, and Middlesex held their position, though they finished some way behind Yorkshire, who were well-nigh assured of the championship before they set off on their final southern tour.

By that time war was closely threatening. The end of the season was dismal for players and spectators alike. The last two matches at Lord's, against Surrey and Warwickshire, were bad enough while we waited for the inevitable. It had been worse at Dover seeing Yorkshire beat Kent in two days. Throughout, a blackboard was being carried round the ground, the details differing but the central message the same – so-and-so to report to such-and-such a depot. Outside the ground the rumble of military vehicles provided a background dirge, and on each day telephonic communication with London was cut off in the afternoon. The West Indies touring team went home early, and three championship matches, including Middlesex *v* Kent, which were due to start on 2 September, were cancelled.

Until those final days the thought of war had seemed remote. Even in the third week in August everything was fairly normal, and more than 50,000 spectators watched the three days of the third and final Test at the Oval. It had been a good season with much enterprising and attractive cricket, in which Middlesex played a large part, with Compton, Edrich and Robertson scoring heavily.

Compton made 2,468 and finished third in the list to Hammond and Hutton; Edrich also exceeded 2,000 and was seventh; Robertson in his second season made 1,755 and his average was just over 40. They carried the county's batting. Together they were responsible for 5,363 runs in championship matches, and 20 other players could not collectively get within 1,000 of their total. Indeed second place was held largely by the batting efforts of those three and the bowling of Sims and Smith.

Sims came right back to form. He was indeed better than ever and took 142 wickets in the championship at under 20 runs each. More important, and a better indication of his value as a match-winner, he averaged only 38 balls per wicket. That would have been just over six overs normally, but in 1939 they were

Jack Robertson, a most successful batsman who was unlucky not to have played more often for England

Nearing the climax of Gubby Allen's perfect fast bowling action. The umpire is Frank Chester, most famous umpire between the wars

Jim Sims, cavalier batsman, hitting to leg against Sussex at Lord's in 1950. Webb is the stumper with John Langridge at slip and the fielder showing his rear view at short leg is surely brother Jim Langridge

Harold Gimblett and stumper Luckes watch one of Jim Smith's soaring hits carrying for six in the course of his 69 in 26 minutes against Somerset at Lord's in 1936.

The Denis Compton cover drive (during the first Test against Australia in 1938): an immaculate stroke of perfect balance

Bill Edrich, one of the game's finest hookers, batting against the Australians at Lord's in 1938 on his way to completing 1,000 before the end of May. The slip fielders are (from left) Waite, Fleetwood-Smith and McCabe

experimenting with the eight-ball over, thus coming into line with Australia. It might well have been the only experimental year, for the change had little to commend it. Eight balls per over may suit bowlers who have ample rest periods between matches. It is very different in a country playing cricket six days a week. It was argued at the time that there should be 21 or 22 overs of six balls each to the hour and 16 or 17 of eight balls. The first premise was correct at the time. In fact it was somewhat conservative, for the average per hour was often materially higher. The second was not. Particularly fast bowlers slowed their movements down between deliveries to make the eight-ball over less wearing. And they had a tendency to go flat out for six balls and fire the last two defensively down the off side.

Smith trailed some way behind Sims with 84 championship wickets, and no other bowler approached 50. Gray's length was erratic, and his 42 cost 31 runs each. Peebles with 39 was only marginally less expensive, while Robins and Allen played so little that they together took only 21 wickets.

Among the supporting batsmen Hulme had an indifferent season. He and Hart each played in about half the matches, their figures modest, and Brown was just marking time. Nor did Price have such a good batting season. Indeed the most useful assistant to the main three was George Mann late in the season after the Cambridge term. He scored well and fielded brilliantly. Smith's bludgeon produced his usual quota of between 500 and 600, and at Canterbury he walloped his only first-class century. When the ninth wicket fell at 212, Smith was three. He added 98 of 116 scored with Pebbles for the last wicket. Rain twice interrupted him, and altogether in three spasms he batted 81 minutes. Three of his seven sixes sent the ball right over the tents which ring the ground opposite the pavilion.

The Yorkshire match at Lord's was very different from the calamitous engagement of the previous year. This time Yorkshire had all the best of the conditions. They batted first before rain prepared the pitch for Bowes and Verity, and declared at 430 for five wickets. Sutcliffe made 175, his fourth century in successive innings, Leyland 180 not out, and together they scored 301 for the third wicket. Conditions were so different for the

H

Middlesex batsmen, that they were put out twice by Bowes and Verity in four hours and a half for 62 and 122. Only Compton with 25 and 18 reached double figures in each innings. They were similarly trounced when the weather favoured Nottinghamshire. On that occasion Keeton broke a Notts record by making 312 not out, and Notts declared at 560 for nine, after which Voce took seven wickets and hustled Middlesex out for 119. They played that match at the Oval, borrowed from Surrey because Lord's was required for the Eton *v* Harrow match.

Middlesex themselves also had some overwhelming victories, one of which avenged the defeat inflicted by Notts. At Trent Bridge Sims, without help from the weather, spun Notts out for 194, and the Middlesex batsmen ran riot, led by Edrich in an innings of 160. Voce that day could take only one wicket for 151, and a total of 512 for seven declared led to a ten-wicket win. They had also the better of a drawn return match with Yorkshire; Compton made his highest score to date, 214 not out, while Derbyshire were being beaten by an innings at Lord's. Sims contributed another fine bowling performance, eight wickets for 32, which put Derbyshire out for 110, and five more wickets in the second innings.

The last great burst of scoring occurred in the last match played. Centuries by Robertson and Edrich headed a run-chase against Warwickshire which produced 525 for seven declared. We were grateful to Sims, when he took eight wickets and, helped by Smith and Gray, bowled Warwickshire out twice so quickly that we were spared the third day. Playing and watching cricket had become unreal. Three days later Britain was at war.

Six years were now to be lopped off the playing life of the numerous fine young players who had thrust themselves to the front during the previous three. For some, including Sims, those years meant the end of their Test prospects. Sims was bowling so well in 1939 that he must have had an excellent chance of making a second tour of Australia in 1940. He and Doug Wright were then England's best leg-break bowlers. The long gap also might be held partly responsible for Robertson's playing so little international cricket. When the war broke out, he was 22 years of age and clearly on the threshold of a great career. During that last pre-war summer Hutton had three different opening partners in the Tests: Gimblett, Fagg and Keeton. While Hutton scored runs galore, none of his partners achieved anything of note. The position was wide open, and at the time Robertson seemed a rather better prospect than Washbrook, who annexed it after the war.

Since the reformation of the county championship in 1895, which ushered in the modern age, the game had changed comparatively little. The over had grown to six balls, the wicket had been enlarged and the lbw law changed. Nothing altered the manner and spirit in which the game was played. If a rejuvenated A. J. Webbe had returned to the county side in 1939, the adjustment he would have needed to make to his play would have been minor. The sweeping changes were yet to come. More were made in the 15 years from the middle fifties than in the previous 60 years, and the character of cricket altered greatly.

In the thirties there was much discussion about the excellence of modern pitches. On all the big grounds, except Lord's, the odds favoured the batsmen greatly. Lord's often did, but there was always the chance of finding a sportive pitch there, as was the case in the Gentleman *v* Players match of 1938. Farnes made the ball fly wickedly and took eight wickets for 43. His first victim was Edrich, who was felled by a blow on the head. When he was revived he was told that he had been caught in the gully, for the ball had brushed his glove on its way to his head. The criticism of pitches was not so much concerned with their true and lasting qualities as with their pace. However true the surface the bowler has a fair chance so long as there is pace in the pitch. The shirt-front of placid pace puts him at a serious disadvantage. Before the war there is no doubt that most of the main grounds needed more pace in their pitches. The post-war tampering with match squares by committees, however, was not justified, and changing the character of English pitches had as much to do with the decline in popular interest as all the other tinkering moves made in the fifties and sixties.

8 Great Years, 1946-7

Unlike the majority of their rivals, Middlesex emerged from the war-time interval of six years with a team of genuine first-class cricketers. Some counties had three or four authentic players and plugged the holes with a motley collection. Some strange characters appeared fleetingly on the scene. One county arrived at Lord's with an alleged leg-theory bowler. That description was 33.3 per cent accurate. The leg part of it was obvious. If there was a theory it existed remotely in the performer's imagination. And bowler was clearly a misnomer. He was said to be a footballer. That was probably so, but there was no substance to the other claim, that he bowled in-swingers. Trundling from over the wicket, he propelled the ball in an unswerving course well wide of the leg-stump, and his so-called short-leg fielders prudently approached no nearer the bat than the equally prudent square-leg umpire.

The early post-war years, while counties were rebuilding, were a period of joy for those accomplished pre-war cricketers who survived the long gap. The championship was won in 1946, as so often, by Yorkshire, while Middlesex were runners-up for the fifth time in succession. Yorkshire, a venerable side indeed, proved how comparatively easy it was for the genuine cricketer. At the age of 38 Bill Bowes, having barely recovered from his experiences as a prisoner of war, which left him little more than a walking skeleton, played two more seasons. Despite the handicaps of age and health he took 138 wickets in those two seasons at only 16.4 runs each. Other elderly pace bowlers similarly thrived. Alf Gover, who was also 38 in 1946, exceeded 100 wickets for Surrey in each of his two post-war seasons. The elderly slow bowlers, much too artful for the numerous immature players filling county sides, enjoyed themselves even more. In

116

Gloucestershire Tom Goddard was rising 46 and yet started the period with 177 wickets in 1946 and 238 the following season.

The time was ripe for Middlesex. Their main batting, in particular, had been formed by young players in 1939, and they were still available. Compton, Edrich and Robertson formed a batting foundation of power that no other county could match. Now Brown, who had been making his way as Robertson's opening partner in 1939, also came to the front. In 1947 these four together scored more than 12,000 runs in first-class cricket. Robertson and Brown made the bulk of theirs for the county. Looking back it is even more remarkable than some of us thought at the time that Robertson played so few matches for England. It is usually considered a great advantage for an ambitious young player to be seen so much at Lord's in the Middlesex side. In rare instances it can be a disadvantage and was surely so in the case of Robertson.

During the later stages of the war he had been stationed with the Army at Bovington, where he had no facilities for practice. At intervals he was called to Lord's, in particular to represent England against the Australian Services, who had a wealth of googly-type bowlers, both right- and left-handed. They were headed by Ces Pepper, an all-rounder who would undoubtedly have played much Test cricket, if he had not migrated to League cricket in the North of England before Test cricket was resumed. Good leg-break and googly bowling present particular problems for the batsman coming into a match without practice. Robertson had to get his practice against such bowling in the middle. An average of 34 in the Victory Series could hardly be termed failure. However, Plum Warner, who was then acting secretary at Lord's, concluded that Robertson was an indifferent judge of where such bowlers were pitching the ball, and so was peculiarly vulnerable to bowling of that type.

That reputation clung to him until he hit a memorable century at Lord's against Kent, when only he mastered Doug Wright, England's best-ever leg-break bowler. By that brilliant stroke Robertson silenced his critics, but only momentarily. Soon the word was going around that he was a second-innings batsman. Even if that had been true, it could have no significance when applied to a two-innings game. Whatever the reason he played in only 11 Tests and his appearances for England at home were limited to two. His last Test innings in his own country produced a century, after which he was forgotten.

At a time of great strength it would not have been surprising if such a gifted cricketer had been on the Test outer. Between the wars that was the fate of several, such as Andy Sandham and Percy Holmes. In the post-war period, however, England were scratching for class batsmen. Many without the necessary technique were tried unsuccessfully while Robertson waited in vain. He certainly had the technique of the highest-class batsman, a model for any aspiring young player. He was extremely successful and such a beautifully fluent stroke-maker that he was able to exceed 300 in a single day against Worcestershire.

The ways of selectors are indeed strange. After the First World War, when England were being laid low by the pace of Gregory and Macdonald, George Gunn was never selected. At the time the two best players of fast bowling were Jack Hobbs and Gunn. Yet the latter did not appear among the 27 who opposed Gregory and Macdonald in the Tests of 1921. There were some curious batting choices among those 27, including more than one known to be frail against pace. After the next war, while the cultured Robertson was ignored, batsmen with clumsy footwork such as John Dewes, who had little more than a rugged method and guts to commend him in top-level cricket, were preferred. Dewes had a major Test tour, to Australia; Robertson had to be content with minor ones, for the 1947-8 tour to the West Indies, without most of the leading players, fell into that category.

In a time of famine, selectors, critics and the like have an odd habit of looking for the flaw in the make-up of an accomplished player, while seeking something good in the indifferent performer. So it was in the early post-war years. With some difficulty something wrong was found with Robertson. 'He's a fine batsman, but he doesn't do so-and-so very well.' With similar difficulty something to favour the ungifted candidiate was found. 'He's not really a class batsman, but he does do so-and-so rather well.' So, the ungifted was the one chosen.

They might with more profit have looked to Sid Brown. He

also was not Test class as a batsman, but he was a splendid county batsman and more valuable than some who played for England between 1946 and 1951. He was, moreover, among the finest fielders in the deep. Brown was a chunky man of medium height, ideally built for fielding on the boundary – much the same as Hendren – so that he could get down to the ball and pick it up while running full pelt.

At the Oval he took one of the great catches which will always live in my memory. He was fielding long-on at the nursery end to a left-hander, who was probably Laurie Fishlock. The ball was struck hard and high towards the scoreboard beneath the gaso-meters – they may properly be termed gasholders, but at the Oval we have always referred to them as gasometers. Brown set off from his position. It was always touch-and-go whether he would be in time to intercept the ball. He barely made it, and at full stretch and bending forward he made the catch some three yards inside the boundary, which was somewhat in from the fence. His impetus carried him several yards over the bound-ary before he was able to pull up. That was a magnificent deep-field catch. It is rather sad to think that, if it had been made a few years later, the batsman, instead of being out would have been credited with six runs, because the catcher had stepped outside the boundary.

That was only one of numerous unappetizing law changes made in the legislation-mad years of the fifties and sixties. That cricket suffered a serious decline in that period after touching the heights of popularity in the first post-war decade was largely the fault of administrators and legislators. They have tended to blame the players for their own sins.

Middlesex in 1946 inherited more than powerful batting from the pre-war days. Equally important was the reappearance of Walter Robins as skipper. At 40 his leg-break bowling was not quite what it had been, though he still took valuable wickets and more than held his own with the bat. That, however, was insignificant beside his captaincy. He was both a shrewd tactician and an inspiring leader, his own game and captaincy based firmly on enterprise and aggression. After having to be content with second place in 1946 Robins, like Warner before him, took

Middlesex to the top of the championship before handing over to one of the Mann family.

Two matches finally left drawn in that championship-winning year illustrate his approach to the game. The first was against Yorkshire at Lord's, where rain so ruined the Saturday that Yorkshire had time only to score 13 for the loss of Len Hutton. On the Monday Robins and Jack Young shared the dismissal of Yorkshire for 187, after which he instructed his opening batsmen that he wanted 150 runs before the close. If they could not maintain the necessary rate they were to get out. The 150 were to be scored at all costs. Alas, at the close Robertson and Brown, still unbeaten, returned to the pavilion with no more than 98 scored. They were met by Jack O'Shea, the dressing-room attendant, to tell them the skipper wanted to see them. He was in his bath. When they started to un-pad, they were told that Robins wanted them at once, in the bathroom. Still padded they received a dressing-down from the skipper, getting what might be called the Disorder of the Bath. On the final day Robertson made 108, Brown 130 and together they made 222, but the lost time could not be made up, and Yorkshire were not pressed in playing through to safety.

The other game was at Canterbury, where Robins played a major part in a rearguard action which at one time looked like producing a victory. Kent, for whom Arthur Fagg made 184 and Doug Wright took six wickets for 87, made Middlesex follow on 198 behind. Robertson and Edrich, partners while 193 were added, scored centuries, and Robins himself walloped 68 with 12 fours in 65 minutes. Kent were finally left two hours in which to make 232 and were soon in trouble at 30 for four wickets. Brian Valentine and Tony Pawson then checked Middlesex, and Robins used his own bowling as the sacrificial carrot which might spur them to recklessness. Having added 95 in only 37 minutes both were induced to fatal speeding, but nothing could afterwards persuade Leslie Todd and Ray Dovey from a defensive course which baulked Middlesex.

Those two episodes illustrate the spirit in which Robins approached the game of cricket. When some years later he was made chairman of the Test selectors, at a time when England's international cricket was being ruled by safety-first tactics, we hoped that same spirit would make itself felt. He intended that it should and told us so in a well-remembered press conference at Lord's. In practice, however, Robins was no longer the fire-eater who had made his own playing career so successful. It may be that the illness which not very long afterwards laid him low was already in its early stages. Whatever the cause, the one-time dominating captain failed to impose his will on Test captains and players, who preferred to ensure themselves against defeat before striking out for victory. That was the opposite of the philosophy of Robins. He struck for victory from the first ball and chased it hard all the way.

Two other stalwarts from 1939 continued. Jim Sims was 42 years of age and Fred Price, who was not intending to return to county cricket, two years older. The amateur, Maxwell, did not quite fit the part as a county wicket-keeper, and Price came out of retirement to keep just about as well as ever for a season. By 1947 the elder Compton, Leslie, was ready to take over the job.

Sims was one of the game's great characters, though the fact was not made as obvious to spectators as it had been in the case of Patsy Hendren. The salty flavour of Sims could be appreciated to the full only by those in close contact with him. His manner of speaking out of the side of his mouth and the content of his conversation stamped him as one of the game's most lovable individualists.

He and Bill Bowes grew up together, in a cricket sense, while on the M C C staff. Their match play was largely in M C C matches, which catered mainly for members. The professionals were there essentially to do the hack work as bowlers. Jim Sims had batting ambitions also, and it irked him to bring up the rear of the innings with Bowes. On occasions he was even affronted by finding himself at number 11 behind Bowes, who had no batting ambitions. One day, having hatched a plot between them, Sims became the number three. When they arrived at the ground and were asked by the team captain who they were, Sims produced a double-barrelled name, having tacked his second christian name in front of Sims. The captain, assuming that he was one of the amateurs, asked what he did, and Sims, correctly, claimed to be an all-rounder.

Since his early days in the county side, acting for a time as an opening batsman, his bowling had outstripped his batting, which was never exactly quick footed. He was batting once with Robins against the West Indies and having some trouble with the array of fast bowlers, who made good use of the bumper. After one over Robins walked down the pitch and said: 'What's the matter, Jim, afraid of the bowling?'

'Not exactly afraid, skipper,' he replied, more out of the side of his mouth than ever. 'Let's call it a bit apprehensive.'

After his playing days Sims had a spell as coach, but that was not really his line of country. He was a conversationalist, not a lecturer, and he was liable to be side-tracked. There was more scope for his gifts as manager of the county's team of young amateurs in August and as scorer for the championship side. He was always sympathetic to young players, even when he disagreed with their theories and philosophy – and Lord's is a great place for theories! Once he listened patiently while young members of the playing staff became expansive on the subject of modern scientific cricket. This was apparently something to be respected far more than the simple game played by Sims and his contemporaries, even if general acceptance of the fact was not reflected in the size of crowds at their matches.

Sims finally got in a word. 'That may be so, but people used to come to watch us play.' End of lecture by the young players.

An important addition to the old-stagers was Jack Young, a pint-sized left-arm spin bowler with a perky little run to the wicket and an excellent action. He could spin the ball considerably and, like all slow spinners who grew up between the wars, his command of length and direction was complete. If there was not quite enough guile in his flight to make him an outstanding success when he played for England, he took wickets galore in county cricket, starting with 122 in 1946.

One important pre-war stalwart had departed, Big Jim Smith, and it was not until the fifties, when Alan Moss arrived, that the loss was made good. The weakness of Middlesex until then was shortage of pace bowling. It speaks highly of their batting and slow bowling that they yet managed to win the championship twice in four years. Laurie Gray was a willing worker at fast medium, but he was better cast as the number two opening bowler than the number one. His post-war partner was the tear-away Edrich, who at the most was no more than a change bowler. They furnished Middlesex with all their pace in the first three post-war years. There was nothing behind them, and, when Edrich damaged a shoulder early in August in 1947, Young partnered Gray with the new ball for the rest of the campaign. In his new-ball role, however, Young took only one wicket. As a spinner that season he took 158.

Behind the front-line players the county had numerous very useful cricketers. Indeed they had so many there or thereabouts that they felt able to afford to let Len Muncer go to Glamorgan, where he achieved very considerable success as off-spinner and batsman. Later the medium-paced Hever and left-handed batsman Eaglestone took the same route to Wales. Lord's was still a fertile nursery in those days.

Among the support players at that time were Alec Thompson, a batsman who could strike the ball sweetly, and all-rounder Harry Sharp. The latter was a splendid utility player. He did not look a polished batsman, but he could be very effective, and his off-breaks took valuable wickets. That such supporting players could produce their best when it was most wanted made an important contribution to the championship win of 1947.

This was virtually decided when the top two clubs met on a spin bowler's pitch at Cheltenham in the middle of August. Gloucestershire were at full strength, but Middlesex had Denis Compton and Robertson away playing in the fifth Test against South Africa. Edrich, who had been kept out of the Test by his shoulder injury, played under handicap at Cheltenham. He made 50 in the first innings as opener, and Robins, in the thick of the fray as usual, 45 in the second. But it was Sharp, one of those brought in to fill the gaps left by the Test players, who rose magnificently to the occasion and who was the vital factor. Gloucestershire with Tom Goddard, who took 15 wickets, supported by the left-arm spin of Sam Cook, started favourites in a match certain to be dominated by the spinners. On the Middlesex side Young took nine wickets and Sims eight.

At the half-way stage there was little in it. Middlesex had made 180, Gloucestershire 153. In his first match of the season Sharp had already contributed valiantly by scoring 14 not out and sharing a last-wicket stand of 37, in which Young brandished his bat effectively. In the second innings Sharp was promoted and went in when two wickets had fallen for 33, both to Goddard. Starting with an all-important stand of 70 with Robins, Sharp proceeded to make the top score of 46. He handled Goddard so surely that all his 8 fours were hit off that bowler, who might have expected his eight wickets to cost much less in such conditions than the 86 which were actually struck. After the last six wickets had tumbled for 16, Gloucestershire went in needing 169. They fell 69 short of that figure, and again they suffered from the attentions of Sharp, for he took three wickets in the middle of the innings and helped Young and Sims to bowl Middlesex home.

Meanwhile at the Oval a comparatively dull Test match was being played. England had won the series, and on a pitch playing easily there was never any prospect of the final match being definitely decided. Much more interest was taken in reports of progress from Cheltenham. Those were days of great popularity for the first-class game. On the first day the gates of the College ground at Cheltenham were closed, and inside was a record crowd of 14,500. How tightly packed they must have been!

In the first post-war season Middlesex finished 12 points behind Yorkshire, the number awarded at that time for an outright win. They almost got home on the post, for they came with such a great final burst that they won seven of their last nine matches. One of the others, however, brought them an innings' defeat by Kent at Lord's in the middle of August. After a thunderstorm on the first evening they did not have the ideal conditions for batting on which the first three Kent batsmen scored centuries. Todd made 162, Jack Davies 128 and Les Ames 114 not out, so that the total was 390 before the second wicket fell.

On the drying pitch Robertson made 104 of a total of 242, but the Kent spinners always had the match in hand. Curiously enough, Kent, their bogey opponents once more, also triumphed at Lord's in the following season and so condemned Middlesex to play that thriller at Cheltenham with the championship hanging on the result. Another parallel was the success of Robertson again. This time when Middlesex were dismissed for 229 he made 110. That was the occasion when he finally scotched the theory that he was frail against leg-spin bowling. Doug Wright ran through the other batsmen and finished with seven wickets. His field-placing, putting the emphasis on containing Robertson while having a wicket-taking field for the others, recognized the mastery of his main opponent that day.

Even after defeat by Kent in 1946 Middlesex could still hope, for they had to play Yorkshire in their next match at Leeds. A win there would have again made them favourites for the title. The old men of Yorkshire, however, were too good for them, and, if there had not been weather interference during the match, Middlesex would have been beaten. Sellers, Leyland and Barber were the run-scorers for Yorkshire, while Bowes, Smailes and Booth took the wickets. Judged on the results of the games between the rivals Yorkshire were justifiably champions. At the first meeting at Lord's they had won handsomely by 73 runs on a pitch so greatly affected by rain that the total playing time was under ten hours. Once more Robertson batted skilfully while all others were failing. Only he reached double figures and scored 38 in a total of 74.

Rain and cold had also marred the Sussex match played during the Whitsun holiday at Lord's for Jim Sims's Benefit. Proceeds from the actual Benefit match were still the chief form of revenue for the player. The reward for Sims from his first Benefit was, therefore, down to about £3,000, which was soon made to appear a modest sum, for organization of Benefits now began on a grand scale. Sunday matches, dances, raffles and various other money-making schemes run by a Benefit committee boosted the takings vastly. Two years later Washbrook in Lancashire gathered in £14,000, and in the following season Denis Compton picked up £12,000. If the financial reward was not as great as he deserved, Sims assured Middlesex of first-innings points by taking four wickets for 45, while Peebles had four for 52 on one of his few post-war appearances.

Allen was another amateur who had left 40 behind but still played from time to time, and on occasions his batting was valuable. The Mann family was represented by John in 1946 and George in the following year, when he was preparing to take over the captaincy from Robins. In that year, too, a young bowler from Woodhouse Grammar School, Ian Bedford, had a startling success, which promised to continue the Middlesex reputation for leg-break bowling for many years. On his first appearance he took six wickets for 134 against Essex in a match at Lord's which produced nearly 1,400 runs. Against Surrey he had five for 53 in an innings, and his victims included Fishlock, Squires and Parker. His success against Lancashire was similar, for in the second innings he dismissed the first four batsmen, Washbrook, Place, Ikin and Geoffrey Edrich, and finished with five for 54. With 25 wickets at 19.36 he finished second in the county averages to Young.

At the age of 17 Bedford was a googly-type bowler quite as promising as Peebles had been. However, as often happens to the very young taking up that form of bowling, which imposes a greater strain on the arm muscles than other more orthodox brands, he did not carry his skill into maturity. At 18 the snap had already gone from his bowling, and the cost of his 15 wickets in eight games was almost twice as high. In club cricket he regained some of his early fizz, but, when later he was called back to the first-class game to lead the county, he suffered from his own excessive modesty. He put himself on to bowl so little that his quality could not be judged.

George Mann's inheritance was a goodly one. The success under Robins had been based on rapid scoring, to give an attack short of pace bowling as much time as possible to dismiss the opponents twice. Scoring rates in the region of 2 runs a minute were by no means rare. Robins, who made 102, and Thompson brought the 1946 championship season to an end by hitting the Essex bowling for 191 in 90 minutes. In the previous match Edrich, 147, and Denis Compton, 235, had put on 296 against

Surrey at fully 80 an hour. Both matches were played at Lord's at the end of August. Although more cricket was played there at that time, there were not the same fears of the pitch's breaking up in the second half of the season as is now the regular case. Whatever other progress has been made in cricket, the quality of groundsmanship has certainly deteriorated since committees started to interfere with the work of the experts.

The hustle and bustle reached a peak in the championship-winning season, when the first four batsmen were in spate. As though enough runs were not being scored by the regulars, an amateur came straight out of club cricket and scored centuries in his first two innings. This feat of Alan Fairbairn, a left-hander playing weekend cricket for Southgate, was and remains unique. He could not keep up that pace, and since he could not devote himself to the game his subsequent first-class matches were few. In that season, however, he figured also in one of the more un-usual hat-tricks at Derby. In the second innings he was dis-missed by Gothard, the Derbyshire captain, when he had made 35. Gothard had previously taken only one wicket in first-class cricket, but with his next two balls he also dismissed both Edrich and Robins. His total bag that summer was six for 244.

The fastest sprint on the way to the championship took place at Leicester in a match of high scoring to make the modern eye boggle. Over 1,400 were scored, and, when at lunch on the last day, which was scheduled to end in mid-afternoon, Leicestershire led by 17 with only four wickets down, a win for Middlesex seemed impossible. Yet in the next 35 minutes the last six wickets were taken for 48, and 66 were needed in 25 minutes. Edrich and Denis Compton opened the innings, and other go-getting batsmen were padded up and lurking by the sightscreen prepared to dash to the middle, if a wicket fell. None did fall. In seven overs the 66 were hit off, and Middlesex were home with four minutes to spare.

Denis Compton was often a match-winner also as a bowler. He had joined the ranks of the unorthodox left-arm bowlers. His off-breaks and googlies could be wild, but he gave them a great tweak and turned the ball very sharply on occasions. He was

127

largely responsible for the swift capture of those six Leicestershire wickets.

They raced with no less abandon against Sussex at Hove, where interruptions by rain threatened to deprive them of a win. They finally needed 111, and 17 were struck off fast bowler Nye's first over. When Brown was then out, Robertson and Edrich hit the remaining runs in 45 minutes.

Of the individuals to whom attention was paid that summer Compton and Edrich, the record breakers, received most. Compton finished the season with two records that, now that the first-class game is so greatly curtailed, are never likely to be matched. He hit 18 centuries and had an aggregate of 3,816, his average being 90.85. Edrich was not far behind with 3,539, average 80.43, including 12 centuries. Both beat the previous record aggregate, which had stood for 41 years since Tom Hayward of Surrey had made 3,518 in 1906. Hayward had 11 more innings than Compton and nine more than Edrich.

Another rather less specific record was set by Compton. In 1938 he had scored a century in his first Test against Australia, and now he did the same against South Africa. The South Africans suffered more from those two batsmen than from any other pair before or since. In four Tests Edrich made 552 and averaged 110.4. Compton played in all five, and his 753 runs gave him an average of 94.12. Of the 18 centuries scored against the touring side that season the Middlesex twins were responsible for nine.

The pity is that they were at their peak at a time of comparative bowling weakness in the counties. The South African bowling also was by no means powerful. It is, therefore, difficult to assess the true value of their tremendous scoring. For instance, might not Geoff Boycott have eclipsed Compton's great scoring, when he averaged more than 100 in 1971, if he had played as many first-class matches? Records depend largely on one's opportunities, one's opponents and on the circumstances and conditions governing the play. This, of course, is not meant to detract in any way from the performances of Edrich and Compton. They, like Hutton in the same period, were capable of great success against top-class bowling, as they all proved by

The Middlesex Twins sharing a piece of fielding by Murray and batsman
Nicholls, of Gloucestershire, who is not worried by the outcome of the
Compton-Edrich catching, for the ball reached them off his pads

The follow-through of fast bowlers Alan Moss (*above left*) and John Price (*above right*) is identical and just what a follow-through should be *Below*, Peter Parfitt pouches a catch at second slip with stumper Murray and Radley looking on

their batting against the then exceptionally powerful Australian attack.

Ordinarily the feats of Robertson and Brown would have attracted more attention. They shared nine opening stands of more than 100, including 310 and 222 in successive innings. Their 310 against Nottinghamshire at Lord's exceeded the 306 that Warner and Douglas had made together against the same county 43 years earlier, and it stood as a county record until Eric Russell and Mike Harris scored 312 against the Pakistanis in 1967. The first four exceeded 8,000 runs in championship cricket, and they were responsible for 33 of the county's 37 centuries. The other four were hit by Fairbairn, who got two, George Mann and Leslie Compton, who scored his first county 100 in only 87 minutes against Derbyshire after Gothard had done his totally unexpected hat-trick.

The nature of Middlesex cricket in this great period is shown by statistics. They had 11 innings of more than 400, were only once dismissed for fewer than 100 and declared 20 times. Their opponents exceeded 400 only three times, were dismissed for under 100 six times and declared only twice. Kent were the declarers on both occasions.

Those statistics indicate that it was not all a tale of batting orgies. Young had a great season. His 122 championship wickets cost only 15.81 each, and, although Sims was kept out of the game for some weeks by a broken finger, he also had 100 wickets. Gray was not far off with 84, and Denis Compton's 57 at 25.26 placed him seventh in the county averages.

There was to be one more triumph before Robins handed over to Mann. Until 1947 Yorkshire were the only county to succeed in the Champion County *v* The Rest match at the Oval. Now Middlesex joined them by defeating their powerful opponents by nine wickets – a final triumph for skipper Robins and a riotous fling by Edrich and Compton. Together they dominated the match, although the knee complaint which hampered Compton in his later playing years was already becoming troublesome. He had to retire hurt on that occasion during the first day, resuming on the Monday, which meant that the 210 he and Edrich scored together were made in two acts. Edrich made 180,

I

in which were a six and 21 fours, and Compton 246 with 30 fours.

If one single stroke deserves detailed mention in a county's history, it was one played on that occasion by Compton. He went down the pitch to a slow bowler, tripped and fell full length. As he was about to hit the ground he swept the ball to the boundary at long-leg. He was a master of improvisation. On occasions he would adventure down the crease only to find he was not getting to the pitch of the ball and swiftly move on to the back foot to cut it. But he never improvised as remarkably as on that occasion.

Despite his knee trouble Compton, with six wickets, was also one of the most successful bowlers. After Middlesex had declared at 543 for nine the Rest were dismissed for 246 and, in the follow-on, 317. So ended what must surely be regarded as the county's most thrilling season. Their success matched the entertainment value of their brand of cricket. R. C. Robertson-Glasgow wrote about Compton and Edrich in the issue of *Wisden* that followed: 'They go together in English cricket, as Gilbert and Sullivan go together in English opera. . . . It should not be doubted that, in the art of giving pleasure to an English audience, both pairs lack rivals.'

9 A Difficult Period, 1948-56

George Mann's career at this time followed much the same course as his father's after the previous war. He also led a championship-winning side, and an M C C side in South Africa with much the same results. Both Manns were at the head of teams who won the Test series, and their individual success was similar. In 1922–3 Frank made 281 runs in the Tests and averaged 35. In 1948–9 George scored 254, including a century with an average of 36.

The story of Middlesex for a time was also much the same as it had been after 1919, except that the two championships were separated by a year instead of following each other. In 1948 they finished third in what could almost be termed a photo-finish. Glamorgan, the champions for the first time, were only four points ahead of Surrey with Middlesex eight points further away. The difference was that Glamorgan won four points for leading on the first innings three times more than Middlesex, all three at the top winning 13 of the 26 matches required of every county. For a win 12 points were awarded, and four for first-innings lead. The four points were retained whatever the outcome of the match.

It was now possible to lose a game and still gain points. The principle of rewarding failure had been established, and in the next 20 years it was so much extended that at length the successful sides could collect more points from first innings than from winning matches. Such unrealistic systems were dictated by expedience. County committees failed in their job of seeing that their employees played positive cricket; and points systems putting more and more emphasis on the first innings were devised to do the job for them.

Meanwhile in the late forties there was nothing wrong with

the spirit in which the game was played. Middlesex remained an enterprising side, after most others had gone over to the camp of those who thought the first object of a game of cricket was to insure themselves against defeat. Under Mann, and for years afterwards, Middlesex had victory as their objective from the start.

Test match calls and a wetter summer prevented the county from retaining the title in Mann's first year. Compton and Edrich, playing all five Tests against Australia missed nine championship matches. Young played in three Tests and missed seven. A wet summer was against a side's relying on making their runs very fast in order to give a somewhat unbalanced attack the maximum time in which to bowl the other lot out twice.

They won their first four matches, and the fourth provided a fine example of that policy's being put into action. The opponents were Somerset, who had 50 minutes' batting on the first evening after Middlesex had declared at 488 for two wickets. Edrich made 168 not out, Compton 252 not out, and together they scored 424 in four hours, a county record for the third wicket. Though the scoring generally was not as high as in the glorious summer of 1947, that was only one of numerous large stands. When Robertson hit a century in each innings of Gray's Benefit match against Sussex, he and Edrich, 128 not out, shared 168 for the second wicket. Moreover Robertson's opening stands with Sharp, who was filling in while Brown was away, realized 95 and 125.

Sharp with an innings of 78 also had a long and important partnership with Compton, who made 145, in a match with a dramatic finish at Lord's. Kent had totalled 320 and Middlesex were 133 for five when Sharp joined Compton. By making 176 together they won the first-innings points. On the last afternoon Middlesex were set to tilt at 206 in 130 minutes, and with Edrich in the van they made a fine attempt. With three balls to go the last pair came together at 203. Either side could win off any of the three balls bowled by Ridgway to Gray, but the latter settled for safety, and no further wicket or runs resulted.

Middlesex beat Surrey twice that year. The match at the Oval enjoyed a finish no less dramatic than the Kent game at Lord's.

This was a low-scoring encounter on rain-affected turf, which so suited Young that he took seven wickets in each innings. On the last day 23 wickets fell for 273. Middlesex had to score 142 at one a minute in the last innings. They seemed doomed when Alec Bedser, Surridge and Laker had the first five out for 39, but in the next half hour Robins and Mann hit 62. There was still much to be done, and Jim Sims did it. He scored 36 of the last 41. Ten were still wanted when the last man, Gray, went in, and Sims had to chance his arm. Luck was with him, for Surrey missed him twice, and he saw Middlesex home by one wicket.

Just as Warner used to rise to his best against Yorkshire, Sims time after time excelled against Surrey. He was not required to bowl in either innings of that Oval match. At Lord's he did not have to bat, for Brown made 101, Compton 123 unbeaten in 135 minutes, Edrich 84 in 110 minutes, and Middlesex declared at 450 for five wickets. The rest was mostly Sims and his spin-bowling, for he took seven for 58 and three for 64 and bowled Surrey to an innings' defeat. Sims also had a fine match against the Australians with six for 65, while his side were being beaten by ten wickets.

That summer Middlesex played their first ten championship matches at Lord's, and for their next 11 were away. The use of Lord's for schools' and services' matches in the middle of the season was now, year after year, the reason for the county's lop-sided fixture-list, which was not to the liking of their members. May was often a month of indifferent weather, and a full home fixture-list then did not encourage large attendances.

Both Compton and Edrich averaged more than 60 for the county, and Robertson, who was the largest scorer with 1,855, was not far behind at 54.54. Brown again topped 1,000, and in 12 matches Robins scored well to average nearly 40. Mann, Leslie Compton and Sharp contributed their quota. Thompson averaged over 30, and Dewes, a rugged, persevering batsman, made 404 in his first nine matches for the county. He was, however, being tried much too highly when chosen for the final Test. His experience as an opener against Lindwall and Miller was horrific, but he was not the only stab-in-the-dark selection for that ill-starred Test, in which England were sunk almost without trace.

There were eight century-makers for Middlesex, the main four plus Robins, Dewes, Mann and Sims. Robins slammed 101 in 91 minutes while Kent were being beaten at Dover. Dewes made his hundred against Lancashire at Old Trafford, and Mann contributed one to an innings' victory gained against Nottinghamshire, and another against Leicestershire. Sims had scored a century 11 years earlier at Kettering against Northamptonshire; he did not make another until this 1948 season, and then he did so against the same opponents, but this time at Northampton.

Young and Sims were again the main bowlers. Young's 93 wickets at fractionally over 15 runs each matched his performance of the previous year. In all matches he took 118 wickets, and Sims also took more than 100. Gray took 60 in the championship and Compton 50 expensively, but Edrich was now of little account as a fast bowler. The cost of his few wickets mounted year by year, and Middlesex at this time may have regretted allowing Norman Hever, no less than Muncer, to go to Glamorgan. Hever was a medium-quick opening bowler who took 84 wickets that year at under 18 runs each. P. A. Whitcombe, a tall in-swing bowler from Oxford, played briefly that summer. A trial was also given to Routledge, a medium pacer, but the need for pace bowlers remained obvious.

In 1949 John Warr of the Cambridge side raised the hope, for the first time since the war, that the necessary reinforcements were at hand. He was a tearaway medium-fast bowler with a poor action but plenty of energy. He was then a very ordinary bowler and a wretched fielder, and still was when he went to Australia in a very curiously selected side a year later. Subsequently he improved his fielding considerably and developed into a much more controlled opening bowler. Then he formed a a good opening attack with Alan Moss, closely comparable to that of Durston and Haig between the wars. He also later solved another threatened problem by his fine captaincy.

His 30 wickets late in the season were important factors in a campaign which ended with Middlesex and Yorkshire tying for the title. In the last match he played a considerable part in the defeat of Derbyshire, which ensured them of at least sharing the championship, by taking five wickets for 36. By then the strain on Young and Sims, each of whom bowled well over 1,000 overs while taking more than 100 wickets, was becoming severe. Gray again had 60 victims at economical cost, and Compton had a similar bag, but at 33 runs each. Except that Allen, despite his 47 years, took 13 cheap wickets – in addition to making 199 in four innings – the other bowling was of little account.

Four Test matches of three days each did not impose such a strain on the county resources. Compton and Edrich played in all four, Mann and Young in two and Robertson in the match at Lord's, where he scored 26 and 121. And that was the last time he ever represented England in a home Test. So, in nearly all their matches, Middlesex were at full strength. Ten players – Mann, Robertson, Brown, Edrich, Denis Compton, Leslie Compton, Sharp, Young, Sims and Gray – played between 21 and 26 matches. Thompson had 14 games, Robins 12, and after the Cambridge term Dewes played nine and Warr eight. There was little need for casuals, but among the also-played group was Fred Titmus, starting modestly with scores of 13 and four not out and bowling two overs for nine runs and no wicket. The next year he was to start in earnest.

The first four in the order were inevitably again the leading scorers. Compton, Edrich and Robertson were regularly leaving 2,000 well behind, though this year their best total, 2,530 by Compton, fell far short of Len Hutton's 3,429. Brown made 1,636, and Sharp exceeded 1,000 for the first time, including 857 with an average of 33.65 in championship games. He also made his first county century against Gloucestershire at Bristol. With Thompson, averaging only two fewer and yet unable to command a regular place, Leslie Compton, Mann and, in August, Dewes, the batting was strong enough for any requirements. Moreover, Young and Sims added run-getting to their bowling labours, and of the regulars only Gray averaged under 16.

If Middlesex, unbeaten until August, had continued their winning streak against Surrey, whom they had defeated in all six post-war matches, they would have been champions on their own. Now, however, the luck turned, and Surrey embarked on a run of five successive wins. After a clear-cut win at the Oval they caught Middlesex on a rain-damaged pitch at Lord's in the final innings, and Alec Bedser, with eight for 42, bowled them out for 94.

Their only other defeat came in the August Bank Holiday match at Hove, where their batting broke down against the medium-fast left-arm bowling of Wood. His seven for 24 hustled them out for 91, and they had to follow on 211 behind. Though they recovered well, Sussex ran out winners by four wickets. Brown had been having a lean spell and was dropped for this match. Since Sharp helped Robertson in a second-innings stand of 138 for the first wicket, his absence cannot seriously be advanced as an excuse for the failure. But in the next match at Canterbury, when he was brought back, he scored 200 in a total of 362 for seven wickets declared and outpaced Robertson in an opening partnership of 152.

The outstanding batting event was Robertson's 331 not out against Worcestershire, which remains the highest score ever hit for the county. He made those runs on the first day, in six hours and a half playing time, at Worcester in a total of 623 for five wickets declared. Although they were without four Test players, they won very easily. Compton's highest of five centuries was scored in his Benefit match against Sussex. He spent two hours and three-quarters reaching 103 with only seven fours. Then he cut loose and entertained the spectators right royally. In the next 44 minutes he hit 14 more fours while adding 79, and finished with 182. There were plenty of spectators to entertain. Although rain delayed the start on the Saturday, the crowd for the match was 55,000, and on the Whit Monday the gates had to be closed.

Robertson and Brown shared their most significant opening partnerships against the great northern counties. They put on 198 against Yorkshire with Robertson making 113 and Brown 88. Against Lancashire Robertson made 159, Brown 95, and together they made 207. Robertson also shared a second-wicket stand of 204 with Edrich at Bournemouth against Hampshire. The other Lancashire game was made remarkable by the two slow bowlers during a Lancashire innings of 304. Before a late batsman had a fling Young actually bowled 49 overs for only 47 runs. In the entire innings he and Sims bowled 95.4 overs, Young taking four for 71 and Sims five for 117.

That season's joint championship with Yorkshire ended the county's run at the top for a long time. In the next 20 odd years they were usually among the middle-of-the-order counties. Briefly at the beginning of the sixties they rose to third place two years running. Otherwise they were never above fifth and sometimes were among the tail-enders. Their troubles began when Mann found before the 1950 season that he could no longer spare the time to lead the side, and soon he ceased to make even occasional appearances.

Robins took the job on again, but he could spare only enough time for ten matches in 1950, and no fewer than seven people led the side at different times. The others were: Edrich, Compton, Dewes, Sims, Allen and Mann. There were occasions when it appeared that several were captaining the same match, one consulting with the bowler, another placing the off-side field and yet another rearranging things on the other side of the wicket. Not surprisingly they plunged from top place to fourteenth. The captaincy was again a problem after Warr.

Inevitably the giants from pre-war days began to lose some of their glitter. Compton's knee trouble, which compelled an operation and put him out of the game for more than two months in 1950, shortened his active playing days. In the middle fifties Edrich's powers of attack dwindled. During his later seasons he was a grafter, and in time his skill at slip declined. Yet his aggression came back to him when he returned to Norfolk to play with much and lengthy success in minor county cricket. Robertson was the only batsman in the country who scored more than 2,000 in each of the first seven post-war seasons. After that he was never quite as good again; Brown began to fade even earlier.

Sims played his last season in 1952, when he was 48. He had taken 1,579 wickets, made 8,983 runs and scored four centuries. His retirement broke the continuity of right-arm leg-break bowling started by Bosanquet, for which the county was famous. Not until Harry Latchman, a West Indian who came early in life to England and who joined the county in the middle sixties, did a bowler of that type play at all regularly. In the meantime such bowling had gone out of fashion, though overseas it remained an important ingredient of the attack. Young went on playing four more years and took his total of wickets past 1,300.

No truly great players came along to replace Compton and Edrich. Since the First World War the county had been lucky indeed to have two such great pairs as Hearne and Hendren and Compton and Edrich. Such cricketers do not grow on trees, but Middlesex were afterwards to have numerous fine players and worthy successors to most of their other leading players of the early post-war years.

Robertson's successor was Eric Russell, a batsman of the utmost elegance. His off-side hitting off either foot and his leg-glancing have long been among the delights of the game. In 15 years from 1956 he scored nearly 25,000 runs, and was then only 35 years of age, with many good years ahead of him. Yet, like Robertson, he played little Test cricket. Perhaps he lacked something of determination, or perhaps he also was unlucky. The latter seemed to be the case when he toured Australia in 1956-7. Australian pitches suited him precisely, and he batted beautifully. He was in the first Test side but suffered a severe hand injury and batted at number 11. When he was fit again, all the batting places in the Test side were firmly held, and, though he continued to play beautifully, his run-scoring could not win him promotion.

Peter Parfitt played more often for England. Like Edrich, he joined Middlesex from Norfolk, a left-handed batsman of robust disposition and an off-break bowler who might have become a complete all-rounder, if Titmus had not been a contemporary in the same side. That limited his opportunities. During his first nine Tests Parfitt made four centuries against Pakistan, including two in the same match at Lord's. His Test future seemed assured, and in Australia he was England's top scorer with 80 in the first Test in 1962. An attempt then to turn him into an opening batsman was a failure, and, because he was not making runs when he went in first, he was out of the Test side. That experience seemed to affect his confidence for international cricket. Though he had a good tour of India and a reasonably good one of South Africa, his early Test promise was not fully realized.

Titmus was the outstanding Middlesex player after the Compton-Edrich era. As a young man he played two Tests against South Africa in 1955, but he did not play again until 1962. From that time he was almost always a first choice until he suffered a serious boating accident while on tour in the West Indies in 1958. The loss of four toes on his left foot ended his Test career, but he so well overcame the handicap that he was soon again one of the finest slow bowlers in county cricket. By then he had played 49 Tests, taking 146 wickets and making 1,311 runs.

In his early days at Lord's on the ground staff Titmus was mainly an aggressive batsman. He was only 16 when he played county cricket for the first time. Then, still a teenager, he became a dual-purpose bowler. He used to bowl a few overs at medium pace with the new ball, at Lord's usually from the pavilion end. Then he would switch to the other end to bowl off-breaks. Eventually he concentrated on slow bowling. At the time, as a result of pitch conditions, most slow bowlers were relying almost entirely on spin. Titmus was never a big spinner. He relied more on craft. Almost alone among English slow bowlers when he burst into Test cricket he practised the arts of pace variation and flight, and, like Laker before him, he had a valuable ball that he ran away from the bat. Such qualities made him a particularly useful bowler on true batsmen's pitches abroad. In 1962–3 he shared the bowling honours of the Test series in Australia with Trueman. Then he had a great tour on the slow, true and very easy-paced pitches in India. His 27 wickets in that series represented slow bowling as intelligent and skilful as I have ever seen. Before his 39th birthday Titmus was already close to a total of 25,000 runs in first-class cricket and had taken 2,396 wickets.

Those three and Alan Moss were the leading players of the next generation. Moss was a fast bowler, who must have played many times for England if he had not been a contemporary of Statham, Tyson and Trueman. That limited his appearances to nine, but he was certainly among the best fast bowlers Middlesex have ever had. When he retired aged 33 he had taken 1,298 wickets. Not far behind him was his successor, John Price, who played ten times for England between 1963 and 1965 and was recalled with much success at the age of 34 in 1971.

Players of the Moss and Titmus generation had their cricket interrupted in their formative years by national service, which took them away from the counties when they were 18. Some budding cricketers doubtless suffered. Middlesex were fortunate in that their youngsters did not seem to be harmed. Among them was John Murray, Leslie Compton's successor, who kept wicket for England in 20 Tests and played as a batsman on tour in South Africa in another. Murray was an enigma. When he played in all five matches against Australia in 1961, it seemed that the stumping job in England's side was his for years to come. He was, additionally, a batsman of excellent class and one of the best hookers of fast bowling in the game. Yet his form in subsequent years was most variable. On occasions he rose to great heights. His century of fine and dashing stroke play against the West Indies at the Oval in 1966 was an innings to last in the memory. In 1957 he scored more than 1,000 runs and helped in the dismissal of more than 100 batsmen. Only Ames had previously done that double. Yet, with all his ability Murray's record is comparatively modest. His highest run-aggregate in a season was no more than 1,160, and, though he far exceeded 1,000 victims behind the stumps, his keeping was as variable as his batting, good and indifferent by turns.

Frequent changes of leadership could not unaided have caused a drop of 13 places in a season. That Middlesex went from equal-first to 14th in 1950 was also to be explained by the absence of Compton for nine weeks from 27 July and of Edrich, suffering back strain, for five from 4 July. Edrich by then was already out of the Test side against the West Indies, dropped after two matches, although in the first he had played incomparably England's best innings of 71 on a broken pitch. Test selection that summer, culminating in the choice of a rag-tag-and-bobtail outfit for the Australian tour, hit a new low. In the four Tests 25 represented England, and no one played in all four. Finally the touring team was chosen to include five novices, Close, who was on national service and largely out of the first-class game, Sheppard, Dewes, Warr and Berry.

Berry was a left-arm slow bowler who took 79 wickets that season. To compare him with Young was laughable, and after touring Australia he could not hold a place in the Lancashire side. Many good spinners were overlooked, Tattersall with 193 wickets at 13.59 each, Laker and Wardle, who were not far behind Tattersall. Two fine batsmen, Edrich and Robertson, were overlooked in favour of the immature Shepherd and Dewes. All five novices flopped in Australia, where Hutton played a lone batting hand for most of the series, for Compton's form was horrible – 53 runs in four Tests. One batsman of Edrich's calibre to support Hutton might have tilted the scales, for Australia's cricket suddenly became surprisingly moderate.

It is true that Dewes had a magnificent run-getting season with five centuries for Cambridge and four in seven matches for the county. But Dewes against class bowling lacked the necessary technique, and guts alone is not proof against Lindwall, Miller, Johnston and Iverson, as his 23 runs in four Test innings revealed. Robertson that season again went past the 2,000 mark, and he was the one main batsman reliable throughout. Brown had a fair season, but he had such a moderate run as opener that he was dropped in the order. Sharp, who took his place, lifted his championship aggregate to 1,255, which only Robertson exceeded. None of the other batsmen had a particularly good year, and the bowling was generally more expensive.

Until Warr was available Young and Sims bore the brunt of the bowling, supported mainly by Titmus, who took 45 wickets but was not yet scoring well. Gray's 37 wickets were very expensive, and he dropped out after playing one match the following season. He was soon replaced, for Moss and Don Bennett played for the first time in 1950 and soon became regulars, Moss after doing his national service.

Moss played his first full season in 1952 and took 95 wickets, of which 88 were in the championship. A year later, when his record was much the same, he was chosen for the tour of the West Indies, where he played his first Test. Bennett was only 16 when he first played for Middlesex, a bowler of fair pace with an excellent and strongly orthodox action. At the age of 19 he had such a consistent batting season that, although his top score was only 66, he averaged nearly 30 and scored more than 1,000. As he was taking around 40 wickets each season his value to the side was considerable, and his future looked very bright. Yet, as he matured he was never more than a useful county player. By 1965, when still only 31, he was tailing off. He seemed to lack ambition, which was unusual in a Yorkshireman born at Wakefield. He scored the first of his four centuries against Yorkshire at Lord's in 1954, an innings which unexpectedly gave Middlesex the first-innings points. A total of 10,656 runs and 784 was hardly worthy of a player with so much ability.

As soon as he returned from doing his national service Titmus took 100 wickets and had done so 16 times by the winter of 1971, when still a year on the right side of 40. In 1955 he was one of six all-rounders who did the double. Altogether he did it eight times, equalling W. G. Grace, Trevor Bailey, Maurice Nichols, Frank Tarrant, Maurice Tate and Frank Woolley. Only Rhodes, Hirst, Vallance Jupp and Ewart Astill did the double more often.

During the two years in which the captaincy was shared by Edrich and Compton Middlesex finished seventh and fifth. In the second year Moss had arrived as a front-line opening bowler, and Compton bowled more dangerously than for some seasons. Together they took 162 championship wickets, while Young took 137. The attack was decidedly stronger than in 1951, when Young and Sims shouldered the burden, and Moss, playing in 15 games, and Compton each took 42 wickets.

Brown was back to form in that earlier year, and, scoring nearly 1,700 in all matches, enjoyed his last really successful season. Against Somerset he made 232 not out and shared two long stands, 199 with Robertson for the first wicket and 198 unfinished for the third with Dewes. At Portsmouth both openers scored centuries, Robertson, 135, Brown, 194, and they put on 232 in not much more than three hours. Compton, playing in half the matches, had an excellent summer, and Edrich was in admirable form in championship games.

Robertson, however, was the great county batsman. In the

championship alone he made 2,542 runs, 2,917 in all games, and had seven centuries. He could not have struck such form at a better time, for this was his Benefit year, and he excelled in his match against Sussex. His sparkling 91 and Compton's brilliance while making 169 in three hours and a half led to an innings win. When Robertson made 201 not out against Somerset on 17 July, after having 75 in the first innings, he became the first batsman to pass 2,000.

Dewes also scored well, but as a schoolmaster he could now play only seldom. The day of the amateur was passing. They contributed little to the later history of the county. In 1952 Knightley-Smith, a Cambridge Blue, batted usefully, scoring 814 runs. Three years later Delisle from the rival University batted similarly and made a century against Nottinghamshire. Walton and Drybrough, also from Oxford, and Bedford were other amateurs played, but Warr was the last to do much for Middlesex.

The 1951 campaign promised more than was finally achieved. It began so well that Middlesex were possible champions after 14 matches. They had won ten times and collected 120 points. From the last 14 games they could gather only 16 points, a win against Kent and first-innings points against Nottinghamshire. They lost nine of those games as Young suffered from knee trouble and Compton lost his form in July. Late in the season Robertson was also less effective than earlier. Though he made six hundreds during the campaign, Edrich was somewhat inconsistent, and Brown was generally out of touch. Thompson's improvement, which brought his second century – 140 not out against Yorkshire – and an aggregate of 1,000 for the first time, could not make up for the others. Surrey won twice, and defeat at Lord's by nine wickets, when Surrey had lent May, Bedser, Laker and Lock to the Test side, was a bitter blow.

In 1953 Edrich was captain on his own, and the team moved more smoothly. For much of the summer they were leading, but again they slumped, for which there were various reasons. The Tests with Australia took their toll. Edrich missed six matches, and Compton missed 13 when he was either playing representative cricket or resting his knee. Robertson, who began in great style and early made hundreds in three successive matches, was put out by a groin injury. When he returned, he was so completely out of form that he was not even among the six who topped 1,000 in the championship games. The six ahead of him were Edrich, Compton, Brown, Thompson, Bennett and Sharp. Dewes did little that year, and Charles Robins, who played a few games now and then, never looked like emulating his father after his schooldays, when he had showed considerable promise.

The end of the season was almost unrelieved failure. From 8 August they lost in turn to Surrey, Worcestershire, Gloucestershire and Surrey, and finally drew with Lancashire. Surrey's famous spinners, Laker and Lock, revelled in conditions suiting them. Yet at the Oval Compton played a superb innings on a spiteful pitch, when he made 63 out of 77 in 50 minutes.

The season began with a tie at Peterborough, where Young took the last two wickets with successive balls. The first of the pair was stumped by Leslie Compton. In such circumstances, when there was a first-line batsman at the other end, number ten must have taken leave of his senses to allow himself to be dismissed in that way.

At this time Routledge made occasional appearances as an all-rounder. His medium-paced bowling achieved little, but every now and then he followed a series of low scores with an innings of merit to surprise even his best friends. He made 121 that 1953 season against Worcestershire, his second century. His first had been hit off the Surrey bowling two years earlier, when his previous best in three seasons had been 54. He batted number nine, and when eight wickets had gone for 129 he and Sims, excelling yet again against Surrey, put on 142. Routledge reached his century with a six. Nevertheless Surrey were easy winners.

Edrich was captain for two more years, and the side was fifth and seventh. Considering that this was the time of decline for the three top batsmen, they could not have been expected to do much better. The twins were contributing less and less with the bat, as the following championship figures show:

Fred Titmus
driving through
the covers against
Hampshire, whose
wicketkeeper is
Leo Harrison

The leg glance
brought Eric
Russell many
runs, and here he
is setting off for
one of them

Charity begins at home. Middlesex players, past and present, on a Charity
Walk designed to help the county's finances, led by Edrich and Compton

	COMPTON			EDRICH	
year	runs	average		runs	average
1954	1,029	54.15		1.381	40.61
1955	590	31.05		1,296	26.44
1956	405	31.15		1,427	32.43
1957	1,404	37.94		1,016	23.09
1958	80	16.00		335	17.63

Robertson was making more runs at that time and holding his form more consistently. In those years his record was 1,292, (29.36), 1,754 (31.89), 1,386 (29.48), 1,852 (37.79) and 1,467 (34.92). Then his batting left him suddenly. In 1959, the year of his second Benefit, he made only 326 with an average of under 15 and retired to become the county coach.

How different it had been at the start of this period, when from 1946 Compton's yearly average for the county had been 61.33, 98.80, 62.66, 50.65, and Edrich's 54.34, 77.82, 60.50 and 40.54. In the same years Robertson twice ran an average above 40, once in the middle 50s and once as high as 65. Middlesex indeed did well enough to hold positions well above half-way while those batsmen were on the way down and their successors had not yet thrust themselves forward.

That Compton did as well as he did in 1954 was surprising. He returned encouraged by a successful Test tour of the West Indies, but his knee gave him trouble, and he also suffered from lumbago. In addition he was still in the Test side and could play in only half the Middlesex matches. In those, however, he revived memories of his greatest early years before knee trouble handicapped his footwork, for he played with all his former adventurousness. While scoring 113 in a Middlesex total of only 194 against Worcestershire, he was going down the pitch to the fast-medium bowling of Reg Perks as though it had been slow stuff. That was the second match of the season. In the first, against Hampshire, he had played innings of 117 and 64 and taken eight wickets for 77 in the two innings. In those matches Edrich also made hundreds. Both Edrich and Robertson made five centuries that summer for the county, and Robertson hit four of his in a great burst during the last fortnight in July. In

K

a wet summer the three stalwarts did well, and as yet the decline was not obvious.

There were certainly no signs of Young's bowling's being in decline. He headed the averages, and with Titmus and Moss did most of the bowling. Warr had not yet found himself, and his season's catch was usually in the 40s, which was also Bennett's usual mark. Moss had finished second in the West Indies tour averages for all first-class games, and he started the new season in fine form. In that match, during which Compton chased Perks, Moss put up a particularly fine performance. Worcester had to make 282 in the last innings, and before the first wicket fell Kenyon and Outschoorn made 159, but Moss won that match by bowling unchanged for two hours and three-quarters and finishing with seven wickets for 101. A good stint for a fast bowler, but it was not as unusual in the past as it would be in the seventies.

Moss did most of his best work in the first part of the season. Subsequently he was handicapped by a broken bone in a foot, which long escaped diagnosis. Two years later injury again checked him when he was in outstanding form. He was chosen for the first Test against Australia at Trent Bridge, but there he bowled only four overs for a single run before he slipped while fielding. He tore stomach muscles so severely that he was out for almost the entire season afterwards. Fortunately for Middlesex Warr was by then able to cover his absence. In 1955 he had increased his bag to 66 in the championship in support of 137 by Titmus, 101 by Moss and 88 by Young in his last full season. Then he took 102 while Moss was laid up.

Groundsmen were going through a difficult period, badgered by committees with demands which changed almost yearly. The craze for turning pitches was followed by the green-tops. Fast, true pitches which catered for the best brand of cricket were a thing of the past and a dream of the future. When the amateur ground advisers finally came round to demanding such pitches, the art of preparing them had been lost. Moreover, the game's administrators handicapped their groundsmen by requiring them to use soils like Surrey loam instead of the hard-setting clay substances. Friable soils cannot produce fast pitches, and on their own they cannot stand up to wear unless kept together by much surface grass. Hence the green-tops, which turned any hack medium-pacer who could hold the seam upright into a dangerous opponent.

Pitch variations could be followed in the Middlesex side. Until 1958 Titmus was usually the leading wicket-taker, and he was well assisted in the previous two seasons by Bob Hurst, a young left-arm spinner and a more than promising right-handed bats-man, though Middlesex made no use of the latter skill. In those two seasons he took 61 and 72 championship wickets, and on the second occasion was second to Moss in the averages with Titmus third. Green-tops were becoming too numerous to please spin bowlers even in 1957, and after two months Titmus had taken no more than 38 wickets. A year later there was so little need of his bowling that in the middle of July his total was only 25. In many innings the bowling was exclusively done by Moss, Warr, Tilly and Bennett. Titmus was established and making runs regularly then. He could afford to bide his time. The many green-tops, which condemned him to idleness, were fatal for Hurst.

Tilly was another who came along at that time among a bunch of young professionals. His experience was similar to Hurst's, for, when the green-tops became less frequent and a better-balanced attack was needed, he also fell into disuse.

It was during this time, the period when Surrey won the championship seven years in succession, that crowds began to dwindle. The 28,000 who watched the first day of the Yorkshire match at Lord's in 1951 became a wistful memory. Pitches which favoured bowlers, good, bad or indifferent, almost inevitably produced cautious batting. Scoring-rates dropped, as did over-rates, and the defensive, negative approach became common, and no amount of artificial law-making was likely to correct the trend, which was driving more and more would-be spectators away. In addition to experimental changes in the law, such as limiting boundaries and the number of fielders allowed on the leg-side, bonus points were introduced. Two were awarded for the side leading on first innings, if that side had scored faster than the opponents. Neither law-changes nor bonus points seemed to achieve any improvement.

Middlesex

Middlesex remained a side aiming to play positive cricket for some years after most were playing safe. A host of new names appeared on the score-cards while Edrich was captain. Some went on to establish themselves. Others looked good for a time and then faded. Among them were Angus, an opening bowler, and Baldry, an elegant batsman who afterwards moved to Hampshire, where he began splendidly but fell away rapidly. Another was Bick, a player of several roles who sometimes played as opening batsman and sometimes as off-break bowler.

10 New Faces - New Cricket

The year 1956, one of the wettest summers on record, began the new era. Batsmen Parfitt, Hooker and Gale, bowlers Hurst, Tilly and Angus, and Murray, Leslie Compton's successor, were pressing their claims. In such a damp season the young batsmen did not do great things, but all three played well enough to make excellent impressions. Ron Hooker was then solely a batsman. Later he developed as a medium-paced seam bowler of great value as first change, and his aggressive batting fell off.

Bob Gale was perhaps the most gifted of all these young players, more so even than Parfitt and Russell, who came to the front two years later. He was a big man with emphatic power in his strokes. There were times when he took opposing attacks apart and looked good enough to play for England. There were others when he looked quite ordinary, and his big innings were often separated by barren patches. Even in the same innings he was apt to be contrary. Receiving two balls similar in all respects, he might drive the first majestically to the sightscreen and play the second gently back to the bowler. Gale perhaps never knew how good he could be. The combination of his flair and the doggedness of his fellow-left-hander, Dewes, would have produced another Bradman. After 1962 he was more businessman than cricketer, and three years later he ceased playing county cricket at the age of 31. He had hit 14 centuries and made more than 12,000 runs.

Edrich led the county through its transitional period. In 1955, when he and Robertson alone topped 1,000 in championship games, Titmus achieved the first double by a Middlesex player since Haig and Robins had both done so in 1929. He also beat Trott's 1900 record of 154 wickets in all county games by four. The attack was strong, the batting unreliable, so that results were contradictory. They defeated the full strength of Yorkshire at Leeds. Yet they were twice beaten by Kent, a struggling side at the time, and also fell to Somerset, the bottom county. In that game on the notorious Bath pitch Titmus took eight wickets for 44 and seven for 51, and yet was on the losing side.

In the wetness of the following season Middlesex were four times bowled out for fewer than 70, by Hampshire, Kent and twice by Surrey, who were now regularly beating them. They themselves put Warwickshire out for 55 at Lord's and Gloucestershire for 69 at Gloucester. Warr had a great match when Kent were beaten by an innings at Lord's. He followed a fine century by Compton by taking five for 27 and nine for 65. Titmus again excelled in defeat with his six wickets for 50 and eight for 60 against Surrey at Lord's. Batsmen had a comparatively lean season, and Edrich, who made 208 not out at Chesterfield, was one of only eight batsmen to score 200 in an innings.

The old order handed over to the new after 1957. Young had already retired, and after that summer Edrich and Compton gave up regular play, the latter mainly on account of his knee. That he played so long and so well after having three operations from 1950, culminating in the removal of the knee-cap, was an indication in itself of his exceptional ability. He was still a fine batsman even when his footwork was impaired. He and Robertson rallied for a final fling in 1957, and Robertson passed 2,000 for the ninth time. He also made his last double century, 201 not out against Essex at Lord's.

In contrast Middlesex were put out for the season's lowest total and beaten by an innings at Chesterfield, although Derbyshire's score was only 153. After a first innings of 102 Middlesex were skittled for 29, and Gladwin's in-swing bowling was rewarded with 11 wickets for 41. However, they in their turn dismissed Kent for 43 and 108 and won by 231 at Dover. Moss took 12 for 59, and Titmus played innings of 62 and 70.

When Warr succeeded to the captaincy in 1958, Robertson had a final season of consistent scoring. Though his highest score was 99, he reached 1,560 in all matches during yet another damp summer. Edrich and Compton also played in some matches but achieved very little. Gale was the only batsman to score a century in the championship games, and he made two. Robertson in the second half of the season was used to bolster the middle batting, and Russell, playing regularly for the first time, began his association with Gale. Their partnership began auspiciously at Leicester with opening stands of 96 and 113. At first their running between wickets did not match their batting. In time, spurred perhaps by the example of Parfitt, who was in the Robins class in that respect, they overcame that failing.

Middlesex had been keeping high in the table, largely because they finished such a high proportion of their games. While others were leaving many drawn, they managed to achieve a considerable number of definite results, winning and losing and so gathering points steadily. Now they failed to do so. The weather accounted for most of their 16 drawn matches, which dropped them to tenth position. They stayed there in the splendidly warm and dry season that followed, mainly because their new batsmen had not yet become heavy scorers. In a summer of ideal batting weather, even if not all the pitches were so accommodating, the highest aggregate was 3,245 by Mike Smith of Warwickshire. The highest Middlesex scorers in all first-class games were Gale with 1,689 and Russell with 1,527, and both averaged under 30. Top of their averages at 34.66 in 14 matches during his first season was Ted Clark, a glorious striker of the ball who in following seasons scored well but never quite to match his skill. Robertson was given a second Benefit, well deserved, but now his batting failed him, and despite the good conditions he never got going.

Yet they won the £500 Guinness prize for the season's fastest 200 in the first innings of a match. At Nottingham they reached 200 for three wickets off 207 balls and went on to make 397 for nine declared. On that occasion the batting really did click – Gale 51, Russell 58, Parfitt 21, Hooker 91, Clark 74, Bob White 54, the latter a left-handed batsman who made more of his off-break bowling when he later moved to Nottinghamshire. Parfitt returned that year from his two years in the RAF. He exceeded 1,000 in each of the next two seasons, and in 1961 his average started moving into the high range.

The bowling, largely done by Moss, Titmus and Warr in those

years, was more than adequate. Titmus did the double in championship matches alone in 1959, when Moss missed ten matches mainly while playing in the Tests against India. Given one more comparable bowler, Middlesex would have had a really powerful attack, particularly as there was first-rate support from the fielders. Parfitt was a superb fielder anywhere, though in later years he specialized in the slips, where his agility made him outstanding. No less nimble close to the wicket was Hooker, who made the backward short-leg position his own by right of brilliance.

The three bowlers with much the same standard of batting took Middlesex to third position in the last year of Warr's captaincy. Moss had a tremendous season. His 114 championship wickets cost only 12.5 each; he was first in the English list against South Africa with nine wickets for 138, and he was third to Statham and Les Jackson of Derbyshire in the national averages with 13.72. That he played in only two Tests was because of the excellence of Statham and Trueman, who together took 52 wickets in the series. Moss played only when a third fast bowler could be accommodated. If he suffered from being their contemporary, he was not as unfortunate as Jackson. Many opening batsmen considered Jackson the most dangerous new-ball bowler among all of them, but he had only two Tests in his career.

Injury cost Gale nine matches, but he and Eric Russell had averages in the middle 30s. In all matches Eric Russell went near to 2,000, and he was in the Players' side at Lord's, where he made 55 not out and 39. In addition to those two Sid Russell, a newcomer, Titmus and Parfitt exceeded 1,000, but Clark suffered from back trouble for most of the season. Sid Russell – no relation to Eric – was a rough-and-ready type of batsman. There was nothing graceful about his actions, but he was solidly determined, and he square cut strongly. Subsequently he became another migrant and joined forces with Gloucestershire.

After long years of dictation by Surrey, Middlesex not only beat their nearest rivals for the first time since 1948 but did so on both occasions. Their batting was consistent in both games, the leading scorers being Gale and Sid Russell. At the Oval Warr and Titmus bowled with much success, and at Lord's the wickets were widely shared, Moss with four for 45 doing most in the second innings.

When Warr then retired, with 956 wickets to his credit, Bedford was persuaded back to county cricket to lead the side. He did so pleasantly for two seasons. The only fault to be found with his leadership was his reluctance to use his own bowling. In the two seasons he bowled fewer than 500 overs in 40 championship games. With full practice his leg-breaks could have been very valuable. One of his more prolonged efforts contributed importantly to the first of two wins against Yorkshire, for at Leeds he took three wickets for 36.

Middlesex could have done with the extra bowler, for though Hooker was now more bowler than batsman and took 67 wickets, Moss and Titmus could have done with more support than he and Bennett provided. More spin in fact was needed and could have carried off the championship in Bedford's first year. After losing the first two matches they won 12, drew three of the next 15 and were sitting at the top. They then lost four of the next seven, and a storming finish, during which Yorkshire and Worcestershire were soundly beaten, could not land them higher than third. Hurst and Colin Drybrough supplied some supporting spin, but it was not good enough.

The batting was on the up-grade. Parfitt, Titmus, Eric Russell and Gale all exceeded 1,500, and in all matches Parfitt passed 2,000, which earned him selection for the tour of India and Pakistan. He scored eight centuries, including two in the match against Notts at Nottingham, and he was well up the fielding list with 34 catches. Hooker that year held 38, and Murray, who was regularly taking the wicket-keeping prize for most dismissals, had 93 victims.

In 1962 the lack of support for the two main bowlers caused a drop in the table to tenth. The strain of this was felt particularly by Moss, whose championship total fell from 112 to 69. Bedford was injured and played in only half the matches. Moss took on the captaincy and did a difficult job well. Yet, when a new captain was needed for the next season, it was given to Drybrough. Although the amateur status was abolished in 1963, the line between amateurism and professionalism having become impossibly blurred, tradition died hard.

The pendulum had swung yet again, for now the batting was eminently satisfactory and the bowling somewhat thin. Parfitt increased his aggregate to 2,121 and was ninth in the English averages. Again he made two centuries in the same match – for Middlesex in a drawn match against the Pakistanis, off whose bowlers he took three more centuries in Tests. His other three centuries were scored in the championship. His Test average was 113. Gale also passed 2,000 and played an innings of 200 against Glamorgan at Newport, while Russell made nearly 1,800 in all games.

They were the main scorers for the county in the championship, but Hooker, Titmus and Clark were close to 1,000, and Michael Smith was staking claims. He joined the county as an all-rounder with the emphasis on his left-arm slow bowling, but more and more it shifted to his right-handed batting. That year he made 650 and averaged 27, but it took him some seasons to make a secure position for himself, after which he and Russell formed another profitable opening partnership. If the batsmen took the chief honours, Titmus still did splendidly with the ball, and his nine wickets for 52 against Cambridge was numerically the top bowling performance of the season.

In their hundredth year, 1963, Middlesex climbed to sixth place, in spite of Gale's ceasing to play regularly. The reason in part was the presence of another fast bowler, John Price, to form a fine opening attack with Moss. The weather was less good, and bowling conditions were so much more helpful that all the county bowlers improved their averages. The absence of Titmus in the Tests was not so much felt as it would otherwise have been. Price with 80 took most wickets for the county, but Moss, 79 at 15.92, and Titmus, 72 at 17.34, were the leaders in the averages. Bennett, Hooker, Bick and Drybrough were the supporting bowlers with averages ranging from 19.8 to Drybrough's 26.87.

The bowling, indeed, was more than satisfactory, and Moss had a fine season before deciding to retire. He was 32, still a key player and fourth in the national averages in his last season. The batting suffered from the partial loss of Gale, which left Russell without a partner. White had his best season for Middlesex, 1,271 runs at 35.3, but he was not a success as opener, and Sid Russell also did not fit the requirements. Parfitt, White, Eric Russell and Hooker scored more than 1,000, but the next-highest aggregate was the 627 of Titmus. The others, including Murray and Clark, did little.

Drybrough's first season was to be remembered mainly by the match with Kent at Tunbridge Wells. On the Saturday Kent were dismissed for 150, and Middlesex scored 121 for three wickets. On the Monday morning only three members of the side arrived at the ground in time for the start. They were White, one of the not-out batsmen, Russell, who had already been dismissed, and Clark, the twelfth man. Jim Sims, the scorer, was also present. By rights Kent should have been awarded the match, for none of the Middlesex contingent was willing to take the obvious course of declaring the innings. Instead Kent took the field, White showed willingness at the entrance to the playing area, and there he stood nonplussed and disconsolate. After a minute or two the umpires took it on themselves to declare the innings closed, judging that to award the game to Kent would have deprived spectators of their cricket.

After the ten-minute interval between innings those Middlesex players who were by then present took the field with five substitutes provided by Kent. Rain on the final day prevented Kent from winning. An expression of regret and apology by Middlesex would have been welcome.

Middlesex clung to sixth position for three years running. Drybrough completed an undistinguished period of captaincy in 1964. Russell had his best season, and for the first time since the early post-war years a Middlesex batsman exceeded 2,000 in championship matches alone. Though Parfitt had a modest Test season against the Australians and also suffered injuries, which deprived him of 12 championship games, he nevertheless passed 1,000 in the other 16. And for the first time he played an innings of 200, being not out for that score at Trent Bridge against Nottinghamshire.

Smith and Brearley followed those two in the averages. Yet

the former was not yet sure of his place, and he was given only nine games in the following season. Michael Brearley came into the side after the Cambridge term and scored consistently as Russell's opening partner. He was to have a curious career, his attentions divided between 'scholarship' and cricket. In the latter field he had sharp ups and downs. His tour of South Africa with the Test side of 1964–5 was unrelieved failure. Two years later, as captain of the Under 25 team, he had a brilliant tour of Pakistan. Some then saw in him a future Test batsman and captain. That was rating him too highly. His true status was that of a very good county batsman. He was also a good wicket-keeper, though after his university days he seldom had the chance to keep.

The bowling was not strong. Titmus, who took wickets galore in August, stood out on his own. Drybrough had one day of glory, when he took four Northamptonshire wickets in five balls, including the hat-trick, at Northampton. Titmus played in all five Tests and missed ten county games. Yet his 101 wickets were 31 more than the next highest tally, 70 by Bennett, and his average was more than five better. He was away when they played Surrey at the Oval and Michael Willett hit the season's fastest hundred in 80 minutes. Price also was missing, for he played in the last two Tests, though he did not have a very good season.

The reign of Titmus was no more distinguished than Drybrough's. It lasted from 1965 until late in the 1968 season, when he resigned. Middlesex in this time had the unfortunate knack of rubbing their opponents up the wrong way. Moreover, their brand of cricket was no longer attractive. Indeed it became dull and stodgy, and the proportion of drawn games was unduly high. Titmus was a much better cricketer than captain.

In his first year they stayed sixth, although Titmus and Parfitt were heavily engaged in the season's Tests with New Zealand and South Africa, and Price was dogged by injury. Parfitt and Titmus, with batsman Russell and Clark, who was in the middle of his three best seasons (after which he retired aged only 28), and Hooper were the outstanding players. Away from the county Titmus took four New Zealand wickets in an over at Leeds. Murray caught eight and stumped one in the match with Hampshire at Lord's.

Hooker, the leading wicket-taker for the county in the championship with 86, had his best bowling season, and four newcomers began to stake claims to consideration. Clive Radley was the most successful, and with the county he was to go furthest in the next half-dozen years. He was a sound determined batsman and a first-class slip fielder. With him and Parfitt fielding there the faster bowlers had the best possible support. The slow bowlers were served by Parfitt, who at the time was unrivalled at short slip. Phil Sharpe of Yorkshire was quite as safe with his hands, but he was not as agile as Parfitt nor as quick off the mark to cover ground.

Mike Harris was another batsman, a much larger man than Radley. For a time he partnered Russell well. Then he was succeeded by Smith, whose long fight for a regular place was belatedly rewarded, while Harris after one lean spell was allowed to depart. Nottinghamshire snapped him up, and there he became one of the most consistently heavy scorers in the country. The other two were bowlers, Latchman and Bob Herman, son of the former Hampshire opening bowler. Latchman was to have as hard a fight for full recognition as Smith. Herman looked a splendid proposition as a bowler of fair pace. He had a fine action, the arm as high as the purist could demand. Because he was not moving the ball in the air, he was persuaded to lower his arm, and his bowling no longer had the same promise.

In 1966 Middlesex had a depressing season. Although Price regained fitness and form and had good support from Wes Stewart, a West Indian who bowled accurately at medium-quick pace, they finished equal-12th with Lancashire. Parfitt stood out on his own among the batsmen, 1,860 runs in 26 championship games; but Titmus had an indifferent season. After playing in two Tests against the West Indies without much success. Russell was also below his best. Apart from Harris, the other batsmen did not do enough to help Parfitt, Clark and Russell. Murray played two great innings against the West Indies, 100 not out for M C C and 112 when brought in for the final Test at the Oval. His contribution to Middlesex was modest.

Hooker, who again bowled stoutly and usefully, had a day of batting glory on a bad pitch at Weston. He went in at 110 for five wickets and slammed 102 out of 120, and Middlesex gained an easy win. Price and Titmus revelled in the conditions to have Somerset out for 158 and 43, and Titmus did his first hat-trick. Hooker, however, was even then troubled by his back, a condition which finally caused him to retire three years later.

That was a year to be dismissed as quickly as possible; and 1967 was not much better. They did rise to seventh place, but their cricket was depressingly negative on many occasions. Yet there were some notable individual performances. Titmus regained his bowling form, revived his flagging batting and did the double for the first time since 1962. Harris was third to Parfitt and Russell in the county averages, and Radley and Smith also scored well. In all matches Harris made 1,715 and was 11th in the national averages. He and Russell set up a county record with a first-wicket partnership of 312 against the Pakistanis, and Russell was the first batsman to reach 1,000 that summer.

Price and Hooker were again subjects of injury, but Stewart maintained his form reasonably well, while Herman had his best season with 68 victims in 20 championship matches. Parfitt's bowling was used much more and more profitably, and Latchman had a day out with seven wickets for 91 against the Pakistanis before the big Russell-Harris stand.

A year later Harris and Stewart faded from the Middlesex scene while Latchman came to the front with 81 championship wickets. There was nothing wrong with the bowling, for Price and Titmus also had excellent seasons. The batting was very different. The scoring was low and slow, so that only 21 batting bonus points were gained, fewer than the scores of all other counties. The new system had been introduced a year earlier to reward wickets and runs in excess of 150 scored off the first 85 overs of the first innings of each side. It was claimed to be a success but, harmful to middle-order batsmen and slow bowling, it was certainly not an all-round one.

Middlesex were plunging to the foot of the table, when Titmus handed over the captaincy to Parfitt. By winning the last four matches they reached tenth position. Though a failure that year as skipper, Titmus as a player remarkably overcame the handicap of the loss of his toes in the boating accident in the West Indies. He had two particularly unusual bowling spells – six wickets for five runs in 13 overs against Oxford and five for 11 in 18.4 against Worcestershire. Moreover he headed the county batsmen – not that this was much of a feat, for he did so by making 846 runs and averaging 25.63. Only Russell and Parfitt reached 1,000, and the poor state of the pitch at Lord's could not be blamed entirely for the general failure.

Parfitt had two seasons of captaincy, and it was a job made difficult in more ways than one. The Middlesex committee, who struck impartial observers as being astonishingly out of touch with the contemporary game and their own team, were unduly slow to confirm him in the position. The impression was given that he entered the fray without the confidence and full support of an ineffectual committee. It also seemed that he could have enjoyed greater support from some of the more senior players.

None of those senior to Parfitt played well in 1969. Russell's batting went to pieces in his Benefit year. Titmus took only 59 wickets in the championship at over 25 runs each and averaged under 13 with the bat. Murray was his usual exasperating self – a man of gifts making all too little of them. Parfitt himself, beset with problems, was not at his best, and the most successful batting was done by Radley. He alone exceeded 1,000 and his average of 40.61 gave him a lead of more than ten over Parfitt. Smith also played better than most of the seniors, and a Rhodesian-born newcomer, Norman Featherstone, was quite the most attractive stroke player. He was inclined to be rash, but that is how many of the greatest batsmen have started, among them Wally Hammond.

Counties were now allowed to register specially one overseas cricketer and play him without further qualification. Middlesex chose Alan Connolly, the Australian medium-fast bowler, but they got much less than they expected. He had no more than an average season in 1969 and such a wretched one the following season that he kept his place only because Herman had gone sadly back. After that he retired by mutual consent without completing his three-year contract. The bowling was no more encouraging than the batting. Price did little, Latchman less, though the fault was not perhaps entirely his, for few captains then understood the uses of leg-spinners, and Hooker averaged little more than a wicket a match. His place was due to be taken by Keith Jones, a hard-working cricketer who bowled medium-paced in-swingers and had possibilities as an attacking batsman.

In all the circumstances 11th place was as good as could be expected, but in 1970 Middlesex plunged to sixteenth for only the second time. The fault now lay with the bowlers. Price, 77 wickets at 23.5, finished top of an unsuccessful bunch. Titmus, troubled to some degree by his knee, took 89 expensively in nearly 1,000 overs. The batsmen were in much better form. Parfitt, Russell, Radley, Smith, Murray and Featherstone, to put them in their order in the averages, scored more than 1,000. Brearley had been reappearing for a few games in the past two seasons, and he also batted with some success. Russell and Smith had their partnership going smoothly, and against Oxford University they had stands of 131 and 140 unfinished.

The committee were now trying to persuade Brearley to return full time to cricket. He was not sufficiently interested merely in a playing capacity. So Parfitt was thrown over and the captaincy added as further inducement, which he took. Parfitt had undoubtedly been badly treated, but in fact the move worked out well. The side moved up to sixth position, and at one time their prospects of taking the 1971 championship were being discussed.

Among the reasons for the climb, and one for which the new captain was particularly responsible, was Latchman's return to wicket-taking form. Instead of being made to feel a luxury to be sampled in small doses when the heavier stuff was proving indigestible, he became a main course. Brearley used him as a front-line attacker, and only Titmus took more than his 77 wickets in the championship. Spin, indeed, on the often bare and worn pitches at Lord's was the main weapon, for to the 102 wickets of Titmus were added valuable contributions by the other two less-frequently used off-spinners – Featherstone took 16 economical wickets and Parfitt took 20. Jones made a considerable advance and took 71, while Price began the season in such excellent form that he was recalled to the Test side. From that point he was more successful for England, and at the end his 45 wickets in the championship had cost over 30 each.

Though Smith had an in-and-out season, the batting was strong. Both Parfitt and Russell exceeded 1,500; Radley with ten not-out innings just took top place from Parfitt with 40.72, and Brearley and Featherstone, who hit his first century, also scored and averaged well.

In 1963 the Gillette Cup had been started; it was the first of the over-limit competitions. Middlesex had their moments in this one-day cricket but have not gone beyond the semi-final. They might have had a better record if they had not so often been drawn against Surrey. They met them five times in eight seasons starting in 1964, and Surrey knocked them out four times. In that 1964 competition they started with a particularly good win against Yorkshire before falling easily to Surrey. In the following season, having beaten Buckinghamshire, Derbyshire and Sussex, the Cup holders, they lost again to Surrey in the semi-final. That was a high-scoring match, Middlesex 250 for eight wickets and Surrey 252 for five. Bennett was often the most successful bowler and Murray a fast-scoring batsman in the early Cup years.

Middlesex did not win another tie until 1968, when they again reached the semi-final, this time taking Surrey in their stride. Russell scored 123 in a total of 220 for eight, and Herman took six for 42 to dismiss Surrey for 117. Warwickshire put them out in the semi-final, and in the next three years they managed wins only against two minor counties and Derbyshire. In 1970 Bill Edrich, then aged 54, returned to Lord's with Norfolk. Though his side was convincingly beaten, Edrich was their top scorer, and such was his aggressive stroke play that he batted only 37 balls for his 36. In the third round they had an even higher-scoring match with Surrey, who first made 280 for five. So well did the early batsmen play that Middlesex looked like getting home until a fine spell of bowling by Willis, who took six wickets for 49, upset them. They finished with 272 for nine, narrowly beaten, and Surrey also put them out at the first hurdle in 1971.

Middlesex have also been undistinguished in the John Player League, a 40-over romp of highly unrealistic and improbable cricket, which drew Sunday afternoon picnickers in large numbers. They finished seventh in the first year in 1969, when Smith made 517 runs with a top score of 103. Centuries have inevitably been rare, but another was hit for Middlesex that year, 133 not out by Radley, and it was the highest in the competition. Smith made his century against Surrey at Lord's, and Hooker, who shortly afterwards announced his retirement, followed it by taking six wickets for 6 runs and having Surrey out for 83. They made the lowest score in the competition, 46 against Worcestershire at Kidderminster, and also had the highest, 288 for six by Sussex, hit off their bowling. In 1970 they were 11th, in 1971 thirteenth and had not yet come to terms with this one-day brand of play.

It gives the very early batsmen the only real chance of shaping their innings, and even they cannot spend long acclimatizing themselves. It is not, therefore, surprising to find Russell, Smith and Parfitt, the first three in the order, finishing the 1970 season with the best batting records. Russell and Smith had stands of 109 against Nottinghamshire and 107 against Worcestershire. In the previous year Featherstone hit Jesty for 27 in an over with three sixes, two fours and a single, in the course of a knock of 52 against Hampshire.

11 A Cloudy Future

People make history, and Middlesex have been fortunate in their individuals, who were able to make their story so rich. They have had their eccentrics, their salty characters and a wealth of highly talented players, who have done much for the game of cricket. Wit on the field, and off it, was exemplified by Hendren. Inventiveness was revealed most obviously by Bosanquet, when he produced the googly. It was equally evident in the extremely individual strokes which Compton grafted on to sound technique.

Team-picking is a fascination hard to resist. I shall resist the temptation and refrain from sticking out my neck by naming a Middlesex side down the ages. But it would surely be an easier task than in the case of most counties, because eight players could not possibly be omitted. Judged on their prime cricketing years, J. T. Hearne and his Australian collaborators, Tarrant and Trott, could not be overlooked. J. W. Hearne and Hendren, Compton and Edrich are similarly assured, and Allen, as the county's most distinguished fast bowler in Test cricket, would have to be given a place. Most people would probably consider Warner to be the captain best equipped to bridge the gap between the different generations of players.

It is after that point that the selector is liable to run into trouble. Who is to keep wicket? MacGregor or Hurrell, or Lyttelton, or Fred Price, or Murray? Probably not Murray, for I cannot imagine that J. T. Hearne and Trott would relish bowling to a long-stop, and by training and experience he is not equipped to stand up to bowling of their type and pace.

Then, how do we assess the giants of the early years? They include C. T. Studd, who did the double twice in successive years when that feat was almost exclusively the preserve of W. G. Grace. They also include Stoddart, who played both cricket and rugger for England, O'Brien and Francis Ford and, going back still further, the fabulous Walkers. Would Studd be of more value to the side than Bosanquet, who twice hit centuries in each innings of a first-class match and bowled Australia to defeat in his first Test? Was Stoddart a better batsman than Jack Robertson? And where does Titmus stand in all this?

Middlesex have a proud history. How much more history remains to them and the other counties cannot be determined. It may not be very much, if the game is not blessed with wiser administration than it has suffered in recent years. One thing is quite clear, that the future story will be of a character very different from the present one.

All should fear for the first-class game, when there are people abroad who advocate squeezing out the two-innings match and concentrating on one-day cricket. When first conceived, the latter was to be an adjunct to the first-class game, but soon it was being discussed as a substitute. County-championship cricket may not be paying its way, but the one-day game cannot live without it. People throng to watch the over-limit match played by cricketers of high reputation. Such reputations cannot be made in one-day cricket, for that there is no possible substitute for the first-class game. The standard of play in the latter is already closely threatened by the conditions of play in the championship and the slap-dash nature of over-limit cricket.

A particular problem facing most counties in 1972 was how to maintain the flow of talented young players into their first elevens. Only a quarter of a century ago the large counties had playing staffs of 25 and even 30 professionals. Now many were budgeting for 14 or 15. The few reserves must all be ready to step straight into the championship side to fill gaps. There is no vacancy on the playing staff for the school-leaver of high promise. Ready-made cricketers are required. How they are going to arrive at that point in the future without being groomed on nursery staffs is not clear.

On the solution to the many problems depends the richness or otherwise of the future history of Middlesex and their competitors. No solution is to be expected from further legislation. The core of the matter is the spirit in which the first-class game is played. Bill Bowes once said: 'We never gave any thought to entertaining spectators. It just happened that the way we played cricket did entertain them.' Given the right spirit, cricket will survive its crisis, and no amount of legislation can influence that. The influence exerted must be more direct.

Appendixes:

Middlesex Landmarks

1864 County Club formed. Dismissed for 20 by M C C
1866 Middlesex rated top county
1878 First championship
1882 C. T. Studd did all-rounder's double and repeated feat 1883
1883 Hon A. Lyttelton and I. D. Walker made 324 for second wicket against Gloucestershire
1887 A. J. Webbe scored 243 not out against Yorkshire
1888 G. Burton took all ten Surrey wickets in an innings, and took 16 for 114 against Yorkshire
1891 A. E. Stoddart scored 215 not out against Lancashire
1893 J. T. Hearne was the first Middlesex bowler to take 200 wickets in a season in all first-class matches
1894 R. S. Lucas and J. T. Rawlin made 150 for ninth wicket against Surrey.
1895 T. C. O'Brien and R. S. Lucas made 338 for fifth wicket against Nottinghamshire
1898 J. T. Hearne took 16 for 114 against Lancashire
1899 A. E. Trott was the first all-rounder to make 1,000 runs and take 200 wickets in a season; repeated feat following year. He also drove ball over pavilion at Lord's
1900 Stoddart scored 221 against Somerset in his last innings for county
1902 G. MacGregor stumped five Nottinghamshire batsman in innings
1903 Second championship
1904 J. Douglas and P. F. Warner scored 306 for first wicket against Nottinghamshire

1907 Trott took four wickets in four balls and did second hat-trick in same innings of his Benefit match against Somerset. A. C. MacLaren, Lancashire captain, refused to continue match against Middlesex at Lord's after spectators had walked on pitch

1909 Gloucestershire beaten in single day

1910 J. W. Hearne took seven wickets for 0 in 25 balls against Essex

1913 First of three doubles of 2,000 runs and 100 wickets by J. W. Hearne

1914 Year of big stands between F. A. Tarrant and J. W. Hearne, including 380 for second wicket against Lancashire. Tarrant took 16 for 176 against Lancashire

1920 Third championship in Warner's last season. First four batsmen, Warner, H. W. Lee, J. W. Hearne and N. Haig scored centuries in same innings against Sussex

1921 Fourth championship

1923 First four batsmen again scored centuries in same innings – Lee, H. L. Dales, J. W. Hearne and E. H. Hendren against Hampshire

1925 P. Holmes scored 315 not out, highest ever at Lord's, for Yorkshire *v* Middlesex

1926 J. B. Hobbs set new Lord's record, 316 not out for Surrey *v* Middlesex

1929 G. O. Allen took all ten Sussex wickets in an innings

1933 Hendren, aged 44, made his highest score, 301 not out, against Worcestershire

1934 Hendren was top of Middlesex averages for the 16th consecutive year

1938 C. I. J. Smith hit 69 in 20 minutes against Sussex and 66 in 18 minutes against Gloucestershire

1939 W. J. Edrich scored 1,000 before end of May. Runners-up in championship fourth year running

1946 Runners-up again in first post-war season

1947 Fifth championship in year of batting records – D. C. S. Compton 3,816 and 18 centuries (13 for Middlesex), Edrich 3,539 and 12 centuries, J. D. Robertson 2,760 and 12 centuries, S. M. Brown 2,078 and four centuries

Robertson and Brown scored 310 first wicket against Nottinghamshire

1948 Edrich and Compton scored 424 unfinished for third wicket against Somerset

1949 Robertson scored 331 not out in a day against Worcestershire

1950 Shared championship with Yorkshire

1955 F. J. Titmus took 158 wickets for Middlesex, highest in season for the county

1957 Dismissed for 29 by Derbyshire, lowest Middlesex total since 1864. J. T. Murray did wicket-keeper's double, 1,000 runs and 100 dismissals

1967 W. E. Russell and M. J. Harris scored 312, first wicket, against Pakistanis

Titmus did all-rounder's double for eighth time

County Records

Highest total: 642 for three wickets *v* Hampshire, 1923

Highest individual score: 331 not out by J. D. Robertson *v* Worcestershire, 1949

Most in a season: 2,650 by W. J. Edrich, 1947

Most in career: 40,302 by E. H. Hendren

Most hundreds: 119 by E. H. Hendren

Most hundreds in season: 13 by D. C. S. Compton, 1947

Most wickets: 2,133 by J. T. Hearne

Most wickets in season: 158 by F. J. Titmus, 1955

First wicket: 312 by W. E. Russell and M. J. Harris *v* Pakistanis, 1967

Second wicket: 380 by F. A. Tarrant and J. W. Hearne *v* Lancashire, 1914

Third wicket: 424* by W. J. Edrich and D. C. S. Compton *v* Somerset, 1948

Fourth wicket: 325 by J. W. Hearne and E. H. Hendren *v* Hampshire, 1919

Fifth wicket: 338 by R. S. Lucas and T. C. O'Brien *v* Sussex, 1895

Sixth wicket: 227 by C. T. Radley and F. J. Titmus *v* South
Africans, 1965

Seventh wicket: 271* by E. H. Hendren and F. T. Mann *v*
Notts, 1925

Eighth wicket: 182* by M. H. C. Doll and H. R. Murrell *v*
Notts, 1913

Ninth wicket: 160* by E. H. Hendren and T. J. Durston *v*
Essex, 1927

Tenth wicket: 230 by R. W. Nicholls and W. Roche *v* Kent,
1899

* indicates stand unfinished

Middlesex Test Players for England

G. O. Allen (25) 1930-48

B. J. T. Bosanquet (7) 1903-5

H. R. Bromley-Davenport (4)
1895-8

D. C. S. Compton (78)
1937-57

J. G. Dewes (5) 1948-51

T. J. Durston (1) 1921

W. J. Edrich (39) 1938-55

F. G. J. Ford (5) 1894

N. Haig (5) 1921-30

J. T. Hearne (12) 1896-9

J. W. Hearne (24) 1911-26

E. H. Hendren (51) 1921-35

H. W. Lee (1) 1931

A. P. Lucas (5) 1880-4

Hon A. Lyttelton (4) 1880-4

G. MacGregor (8) 1890-3

F. G. Mann (7) 1948-9

F. T. Mann (5) 1922-3

L. J. Moon (4) 1905-6

E. A. Moss (9) 1954-60

J. T. Murray (21) 1961-7

T. C. O'Brien (5) 1884-96

G. A. E. Paine (4) 1934-5

P. H. Parfitt (34) 1961-9

I. A. R. Peebles (13) 1927-31

J. S. Price (14) 1963-71

W. F. Price (1) 1938

J. D. Robertson (11) 1947-52

R. W. V. Robins (19) 1929-37

J. M. Sims (4) 1935-6

C. I. J. Smith (5) 1934-7

G. T. S. Stevens (10) 1922-30

A. E. Stoddart (16) 1887-98

C. T. Studd (5) 1882-3

G. B. Studd (4) 1882-3

F. J. Titmus (49) 1955-68

A. E. Trott (5) 1894-9

G. F. Vernon (1) 1883

P. F. Warner (15) 1899-1912

J. J. Warr (2) 1951

A. J. Webbe (1) 1879

J. A. Young (8) 1947-9

Middlesex Test Players

Lucas played also for Surrey and Essex; only one season for Middlesex. Trott played three times for Australia before joining Middlesex and twice afterwards for England against South Africa. Paine represented England after joining Warwickshire.

Numerals in brackets indicate number of Tests played

Index

171

Index

Index